Public Space

DESIGN, LAYOUT AND MANAGEMENT OF PUBLIC OPEN SPACE IN ROTTERDAM

Edited by
Johan Goossens, Anja Guinée and Wiebe Oosterhoff

Public Space

DESIGN, LAYOUT AND MANAGEMENT OF PUBLIC OPEN SPACE IN ROTTERDAM

010 Publishers, Rotterdam 1995

Foreword

Recent decades have seen an increasing amount of governmental interest in public open space. Since 1974, Rotterdam City Council has had a separate portfolio for, in the beginning, public verdure and, later, for public open space.

Originally, governmental interest in open space was translated into a collaborative relationship among departments involved in the design, realization, and management of open space. In 1993 the level of aspiration for the approach to, and the quality of, open space was set down in a plan for all open-space areas in Rotterdam: the *Rotterdam Policy Plan for Public Open Space.* Subsequently, this plan has been elaborated for parts of the city in the form of open-space policy plans for several submunicipalities.

The issue is not simply one of ambitions on paper, however. Beginning in 1990, each year extra funds have been made available, through investment programs, for the realization of public open space: all in all, a total of 74 million guilders.

Now that all conditions for an effective approach to planning and realizing public space appear to have been met, the moment has come to record the results of recent years. This book, however, contains more than just results: it also provides background information and detailed documentation of individual projects. Here is a book for everyone interested in architecture, urban planning, and the design and realization of public open space.

Herman van de Muijsenberg
Alderman for Environment and Public Open Space, Traffic and Transportation

the previous chapter show that the restructuring operation is not limited to one borough or one submunicipality, but that it applies to the entire urban area of Rotterdam. The vertexes and compact-city policies have been initiated, formulated, and committed to paper by Rotterdam City Council. Large park areas are the administrative responsibility of submunicipalities. Despite evidence that these park areas and their facilities have a more than local, and perhaps even regional, import, submunicipal administrations often tend to think in local terms. In contrast to what the city council can do in urban areas with important economic functions - port, city center, office and business sites - it does

not have enough clout to intervene in submunicipal policies on verdure. To this day, the situation is one that fails to produce the decisive and lucid administrative action desired by all. The vicissitudes surrounding Kralingse Woods serve as an illustration: when contributing investment and re-structuring funds needed for the betterment of woodland, the city council gets a warm welcome from the submunicipality. When it comes to drawing up concrete programs, however, the submunicipality has all the author-ity. Urban programs such as rock festivals, gathering spots for gays, or horse shows prove difficult to schedule in Kralingse Woods.

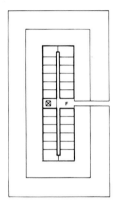

1.

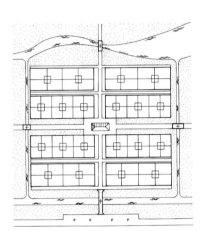

2.

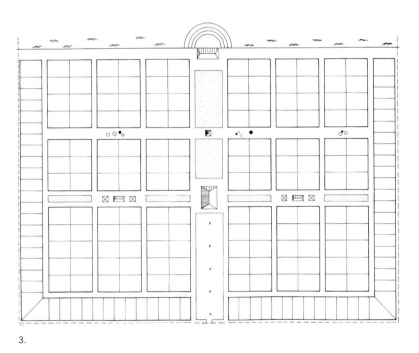

3.

Model of future allotment gardens in three categories (2010), Allotment Gardens and Physical Planning in Rotterdam, 1993.
1. vegetable gardens within the housing environment
2. allotment gardens within the city's green matrix
3. high-quality recreational gardens within the regional green matrix

RESTRUCTURING OF EXISTING PARKS

Kralingse Woods

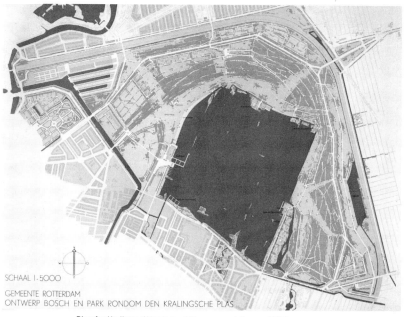

Plan for Kralingse Woods by Bijhouwer and Koops, 1932.

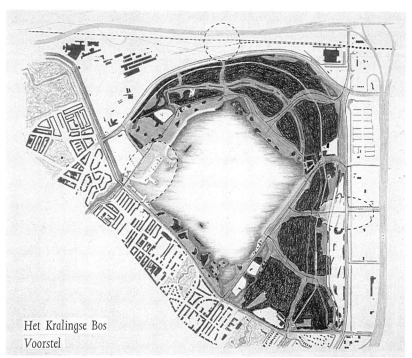

Het Kralingse Bos
Voorstel

Concept of the Integral Structure Plan for Public Open Space: Kralingse Woods, 1992.

At the beginning of the century, working-class families living in high-density districts of Rotterdam had few opportunities to spend a day enjoying outdoor recreational activities. Therefore, in 1936 a 'Dutch Forest Landscape' was realized around an existing peat-bog lake at the edge of the city. Designed by architect Granpré Molière and landscape architect Bijhouwer, the park is characterized by its lucid organization and optimal provision of activities. On the banks of the lake, spacious lawns with groups of trees offer visitors the chance to picnic, sunbathe, or relax after swimming or rowing. The surrounding woodland provides shelter, forms a backdrop for the playing fields, and welcomes strollers to discover the many parallel paths that typify its design. Walking along these paths, the visitor has a constantly changing view of playing fields and lake, thanks to wedge-shaped areas left open in the design.
Through the years, Kralingse Woods has assumed another face. The residents of

Rotterdam now use this woodland area differently than they did when it was first created; they go more often, for shorter periods, at various times of the day and week, and for a diversity of activities. Kralingse Woods has evolved from a peaceful park at the edge of the city into a centrally located green area with a high usage level. The many activities and facilities offered are the source of numerous conflicts within the limited space available. For example, it would be advantageous to make the park more accessible to slow traffic arriving from eastern districts, but the long, narrow golf course between these districts and the woodland poses a stumbling block. An increase in motorized traffic in the woods is a hindrance to pedestrians and cyclists, but getting there by car is important to those who have trouble walking. Visitors enjoy 'nature' in the woods, but the development of an ecological conscience is hard to reconcile with intensive recreational activity. Another problem is that Kralingse Woods is in bad condition as a result of overdue maintenance. The spatial design has fallen into disrepair: there are holes in the woodland mass,

and open wedges have grown shut. Woodland parcels present a sorry sight, the consequence of inferior soil and poor management in the past.

In the eyes of the city council, whose job it is to finance the restoration of this area, Kralingse Woods holds importance for the entire city. Therefore, as one of the vertexes of the city, it must be easily accessible and must offer accommodations for urban activities such as rock concerts. An integral structure plan for the future development of Kralingse Woods has as its objective the satisfaction of various user requirements, as well as the creation of space for natural resources. The woodland must be made to fit more easily into the urban structure, and its original spatial contrasts must be restored. The administrative responsibility for Kralingse Woods is, for the most part, the task of the submunicipality of Kralingen-Crooswijk, which views 'Kralinger Hout' primarily as a woodland area for its own residents. Its council gives no priority to increased accessibility for those from other districts and has reservations about adaptations aimed at accommodating large-scale public events.

RESTRUCTURING OF EXISTING PARKS

Zuiderpark

In the prewar expansion plan for Rotterdam South, a large park was projected for the transitional area between city and countryside. Postwar plans, however, shifted the park northward, between the old city and new expansion areas, so that it would also benefit the residents of existing districts with little verdure. Zuiderpark (Southern Park) was developed along with the modern districts of Zuidwijk, Pendrecht, and Lombardijen. This simultaneous development meant that the program of functions for the park was influenced greatly by the standards of *De 8 en Opbouw*. The layout of the park was closely related to that of the housing projects. In the series block verdure, neighborhood verdure, district verdure, and borough verdure, the park is the facility at the top of the scale. Because the size of the program, which was calculated according to standards for verdure, exceeded the available area of 250 hectares, in allocating space, a choice had to be made between private facilities - such as sports fields, allotment gardens, and gardens for school children - and public park facilities, such as sunbathing areas and water. Partly owing to the influence of the Council of Physical Education, facilities for schools and clubs were given priority. The park design is fairly simple. Various recreational complexes lie within areas bordered by woodland. Within these woodland borders, which together form continuous zones, lie public roads and paths, all of which creates an illusion of one large woodland park. Roads within the woodland zones are connected to the main road, also provided with greenery, that lends access to the surrounding districts.

Zuiderpark has always been appreciated for its contribution to the quality of life in Rotterdam South. Various developments have made it impossible, however, for the park to continue existing for the next 40 years without intervention. In the first place, a sharp increase in construction has made the park less accessible and has had a negative effect on its woodland character. Where once a few small, individual buildings stood here and there in the woods, now closed facades can be seen at certain places along the edge of the park. In particular, the construction of the Ahoy' sports and exhibition complex took up a huge green area, leaving a long rear facade facing the park. Second, retrenchment in the 1980s led to adaptations in the layout and management of the park. In order to have less area to mow, lawns were reduced in size by planting trees along their outer edges. At the same time, narrow and often thin woodland borders around allotment gardens and sports fields were also reinforced. In addition, maintenance was intensified. In the early '90s, a maintenance system geared to increase the ecological quality of the park represented the perfect extension of this idea. Adaptations have not succeeded, however. Because new vegetation consists of groups of trees of the same species instead of mixed woodland shrubbery, the plan has not solved the problem of increasing death among large trees in aging woodland borders. And third, the present multiform population of the surrounding districts no longer has the same recreational needs as the working-class families who lived there when the park was first laid out. Schools and clubs are no longer the organizations designated to give everyone an opportunity for outdoor activity, and only a small number of allotment gardens belong to people who live in neighborhoods close to the park. There now exists a need for public space that can be used for a variety of activities.

In addition to the diminished spatial quality of the park and the need for a revision of its functions, there is another urgent reason to consider the future of Zuiderpark. The park is increasingly threatened by the negative effect of new claims, three of which are the projected extension of the Ahoy' complex, the need for a metro line to cross the park, and a demand for new housing in the area. The city council and the submunicipality of Charlois agree that Zuiderpark must remain a park serving all of Rotterdam South. Each supports a different strategy, however. The submunicipal administration wants the present character of the park to change as little as possible. They do not see the somewhat indifferent spatial structure as a disadvantage, but rather as an advantage. If Ahoy' is extended onto an allotment-garden or sports-complex site, they are willing to allocate another spot in the park to that facility. In the eyes of the city council, Zuiderpark will be more valuable in the future if the quality of its design is enhanced and more public space is created. The latter can be realized by moving private functions to other green areas. The city council sees a centrally located Zuiderpark, easily accessible via a network of highways and public transportation, as one of the city's four green vertexes. The potential extension of Ahoy' must be seized as a chance to create unity in the park and to give it a main facade.

Whether or not the point of departure should be to give the park a simple 'neighborhood' character or to transform it into something more spatially and functionally exceptional, the task is to formulate, as soon as possible, an active policy that will steer developments in the right direction and heighten overall appreciation of Zuiderpark. Otherwise, it seems inevitable that this urban area of green open space will continue to disintegrate.

27

Botlekpark

Scottish Highlanders.

Wedged between the Nieuwe Waterweg and the Botlek, Botlekpark most resembles a remnantal strip. On the north side, ships glide past; on the south side, the AVR waste-processing company casts its shadow across the park. For the benefit of surrounding industry, two large pipeline roads, which require frequent excavation, run straight through the park. Two nautical beacons necessitate a low level of vegetation on part of the site.

The formerly planned cultural arrangement of the park suggested intensive use. However, there are parks with a similar layout in the neighborhood of Rozenburg, and Botlekpark, on its isolated site, was badly neglected. Its only visitors were people taking a walk along the river. The decision was made to convert the area into a nature park. In order to encourage the ecological development of the vegetation, individual groups of trees were planted, open places in the woods cleared, and the edges of the boscages made irregular. Pruned branches were stacked in rows. Furthermore, Scottish Highlanders were introduced as a balance factor. Their grazing and excremental behavior will bring even more variety into the vegetative situation, further increasing the flora and fauna in the park. To speed up the development of the woods, areas will continue to be thinned out at intervals. Keeping Highlanders requires a whole series of organizational and managerial measures. Fences have been placed with small gates and cattle guards at the entrances; a watering place has been added and an enclosure, or corral, built. During hot summers the watering place will be kept filled, and extra provender will be provided in very cold weather. The leased animals will be inspected by a veterinarian at regular intervals.

The park no longer looks like a place where playing fields belong. The opportunity to take a walk, however, still exists. Strolling on a continuous path along the water, one sees the contrast between industry and ships on the one side, and the verdant tree-filled meadow on the other. In the domain ruled by the Highlanders, the experience of nature presides. Owing to very tall grasses and herbs, the newly designed park is fairly inaccessible outside the paths. As time goes on, large areas will emerge that have been grazed bare.

RESTRUCTURING OF EXISTING PARKS

Oostvoornse Meer and the coast of the North Sea.

Regionalization of the Green Matrix

Rotterdam lies in the south wing of the Randstad, an area already urbanized to such an extent that urban activities are no longer concentrated in built-up cores but are also spread out along the growing network of highways and railroad lines outside the cities. In addition to industrial sites on the urban periphery, such as the Spaanse Polder and Noord-West, businesses also opt for easily accessible locations between the cities. Rotterdammers looking for recreation go en masse to the coast of Voorne or to the lake vicinity of the Rottemeren, but they also go shopping in large furniture halls and garden centers found in strips along regional highways. People who work in Rotterdam live not only in the city and its suburbs but also in bungalows lining country

roads and in the expansion districts of Bergschenhoek and Spijkenisse. Under urban pressure, even agriculture tends to assume a more urban, industrial character. Particularly in the area bordered by Rotterdam, Delft, and Zoetermeer, land-related production is ceding more and more space to greenhouses. The result of this uncontrolled urbanization of the countryside is that spatial contrasts fade, that the original landscape becomes fragmented, and that peripheral areas become crowded with marginal activities. The result is degeneration.

Former Buffer Policy

In the 1960s the central government established a buffer

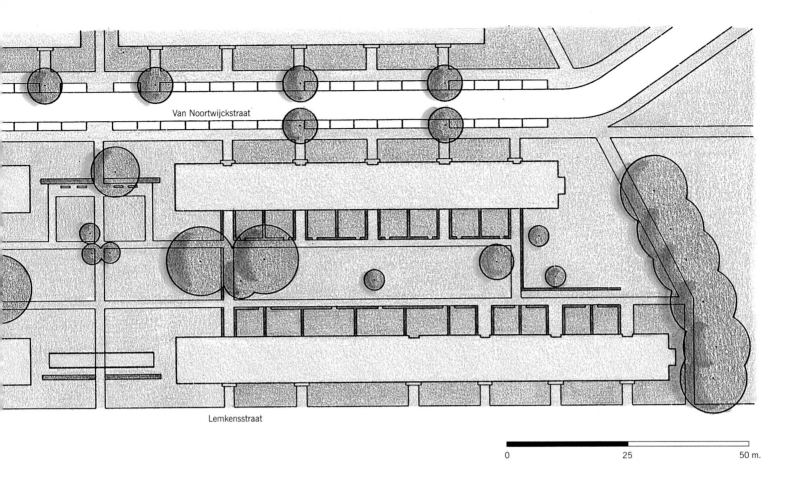

Van Noortwijckstraat

Lemkensstraat

0   25   50 m.

areas of open space. At the district level, the green matrix consists of a centrally located park linked to green zones. These zones, consisting of lawns, trees, and water, run through the neighborhoods like green arteries to the edge of the district. Along the Delfshavense Schie lies a park zone meant to buffer noise and reduce odor produced downwind by industry in the Spaanse Polder. Courtyards in Welschen are linked to green zones. The former were designed by landscape architect Boer as communal gardens. Walking down poplar-lined streets, distant views of a park-like landscape can be glimpsed. Rows of shrubbery around housing blocks in each neighborhood form green plinths along streets and courtyards. The years have damaged the image of open space, owing to subsidence and to the increase in motorized traffic. At the expense of the green plinths, parking places were installed at right angles to housing blocks. And because of problems caused by breaking branches and root damage to the surface of the roads, many large poplars were chopped down.

The approach to Welschen is based on restoring the original coherence that linked urban planning, architecture, and open-space design. The urban-planning

concept has been maintained, and apartments have been renovated and adapted to current requirements. Nevertheless, not all original relationships are the same as they were. A very significant change is the result of a wish expressed by residents to have individual, private gardens in the courtyards. A decision was made to situate these gardens against facades on both sides of public courtyards and to preserve the communal garden in the middle. By rearranging the layout of the housing blocks, various types of housing were realized: corner units for senior citizens, one-story apartments on the top floor, and three-story maisonettes beneath them. Of each two maisonettes, one has access to a private garden via a staircase and the other to the communal garden. An idea to allow newly designed communal gardens to remain open on the short sides, and thus to go on forming a transition to the green zones, had to be abandoned. Wanting to prevent dogs from entering their gardens, the residents asked to have the gardens separated from the communal area by fences. To restore the uniform image of courtyard and housing block, street furniture and garden fences are coordinated to match balcony parapets. Gardens are further separated by privet hedges, which are

maintained by the housing association. A second significant change is based on a desire for a bit of variety and a breath of fresh air in the rather large and monotonous housing complex. An uninterrupted view from the neighborhood to the Schie was thought to be an addition that would lend a special quality to Welschen. To acquire the space for such a view without making a big hole in existing development, the ends of two blocks were torn down and two other blocks extended. The panorama is accentuated by the concrete skeleton of a demolished apartment building. It remains standing as a monument to the modern, industrial building method once developed to provide many people, as quickly as possible, with good housing in Welschen.

Within the framework of neighborhood renewal, streets have not gone unnoticed. Fewer dwellings, along with the realization of housing for senior citizens, have led to a subsequent decrease in the number of parking spaces needed. Rightangled parking has been converted to parallel parking and the green plinth along the facade restored. Streets, all with identical dimensions, have allowed a kind of pattern to develop, which consists of sidewalk, shrubbery, refuse container, and parking space.

Project sites for Integral Plan Noordrand Rotterdam (IPNR) and Berkel en Rodenrijs/Bergschenhoek (2B3), 1995.

Urban Expansion and Landscape Development

When we look at urbanization possibilities for city and region, and apply them to the south wing of the Randstad, we notice a number of tendencies. There is an enormous supply of housing locations outside the cities. These locations are no longer linked to one city but are part of an urban field composed of several large and medium-sized cities. In the period between 1995 and 2005, 25,000 dwellings must be built in such locations around Rotterdam, and new industrial and port sites must be realized here as well. Such developments are not autonomous; they will accompany expansion of the highway infrastructure and continuing differentiation of the railroad infrastructure, including the introduction of new public-transportation systems such

as Randstadrail, TramPlus, and the high-speed railroad line. These urban programs will bring a remarkable change to what has always been an open agrarian landscape. In the past, there was a clearly defined boundary between city and countryside. Many a peripheral municipality or suburb derives its identity and qualities from its location close to the city, but still surrounded by countryside. However, urbanization of the rural area and the low density of development in urban-expansion areas will cause boundaries separating the two to fade.

Merging of the region around The Hague with that of Rotterdam means a multifaceted task for housing sites. Not only must a good general structure be realized at district and borough levels; work must also be done on the new general structure of the border area of Randstad's south wing. Consequently, an open-space strategy is needed on two scales. The problem facing the south wing of the Randstad is the realization of an urban network based on infrastructural lines combined with zones of verdure: green urban expansion. The existing landscape looks like a logical foundation on which to realize a new urban-space structure. In addition, urban interventions offer new opportunities to reinforce the local and regional structure of urban space. A description of several recently constructed housing projects will elucidate the way in which this search for structure transpires within a context of increasingly less governmental direction and increasingly more influence from investors and administrative reorganization.

Changing Plan Development in Rotterdam's Urban Expansion

The chapter *From Garden Village to Garden City* sketches the development of postwar urban expansion up to and including the district of Ommoord. Characteristic of this expansion was the important role taken by the municipal government in the entire planning process. The municipality was responsible for the master plan, the municipality purchased the land, the municipality supervised development of subplans, the municipality provided for open space, and the municipality had a great deal to do with public housing. Districts were laid out according to urban-planning models that took into consideration traffic systems, walking distances, centralized facilities, and the position of a site in relation to both borough and city. Use of these models led to autonomous plans for residential districts; such plans included beltways, quadrants, centrally located shopping centers, and cycle paths running independent of other routes. Links to the surrounding (urban) landscape were not a major issue, and the urban plan made very little use of the underlying landscape.

In the 1970s, trends in open-space planning within urban-expansion projects began to change: landscape was discovered as a mainstay of quality for new districts. The district of Zevenkamp marked this turning point. Just as its predecessors, this project was developed on a raised site. The most prominent elements in the underlying landscape were included in the new situation. Elevated clay ridges from the historical polder landscape were converted into dikes, and the polder canal, Ommoordse Tocht, was also featured in the new district. A shopping center and Zevenkamp's district park are located at the junction connecting these two natural elements. In the 1980s, Zevenkamp was the first district to include former elements of the landscape. Further discussion of the use of landscape in residential districts, on various scales, is based on the recently realized district of Prinsenland and on plans for residential areas still to be developed on Rotterdam's northern periphery – Integral Plan Noordrand Rotterdam (IPNR) and the plan for the Municipalities of Berkel en Rodenrijs and Bergschenhoek (2B3).

WKWR Standards as a Resource for Open-Space Planning

The WKWR standards developed in the 1970s are still working wonders, especially in the area of politics and in the economic sector. Thanks to WKWR, Prinsenpark was given to Prinsenland as a gift. Designers were able to take advantage of a fortunate circumstance: within the total expansion area of Alexanderpolder, the realization of which began in the 1960s, a normative claim for a borough park remained to be honored. The lake in the IPNR represents the same kind of donation. According to standards for verdure, the existing Zestienhoven Park filled the role of borough park for densely developed urban-renewal districts in Rotterdam West. Since the IPNR is based on development of more than half of Zestienhoven Park, from a normative point of view, this park is due to be replaced by another open-space function at borough level. In the IPNR, this requirement has been translated into a centrally located lake.

The district of Zevenkamp was developed in an orthodox manner, according to WKWR standards. Strictly followed standards for verdure were applied to block, neighborhood, and district greenery. The district park is centrally located. Neighborhood parks - playing fields and playgrounds - are found throughout the neighborhoods. Playtime areas for the youngest residents separate housing blocks, forming block verdure. WKWR standards were applied quite differently in Prinsenland. The hierarchical translation was abandoned here. Normatively available green acreage has been combined and used to realize a few larger open-space elements important to the entire district, such as lake and park. This trend is continued in recent plan development for IPNR and 2B3. These plans also combine available green acreage and translate it, spatially, into large continuous areas of verdure. Such areas are characterized by their significance at the district, as well as the regional, level.

The Existing Landscape as a Mainstay of Quality

The existing landscape was a logical point of departure for the urban-planning development of Prinsenland. Differences in elevation, the fan-shaped peat-bog area, country roads, and the existing cemetery were preserved and given new functions in the future residential district. Certain features were converted; others received supplementary elements. The lowest part of the border between the high peat-bog area and lowlying reclaimed land is used for water storage. The broad end of the lake forms an entrance to the district and its shopping center. The pattern of ditches in the fan of peat bogs was preserved, and land parcels between the ditches were allocated for housing. Country roads – backbones of ribbon development – serve as routes for slow-moving traffic and as access roads into the district's neighborhoods. Existing agrarian buildings were maintained, given new functions, and, on parcels between ditches, supplemented with the addition of villas and informal urban functions such as garden centers and manèges. The cemetery was integrated into the park. Existing elements of the landscape form a basis for Prinsenland's green

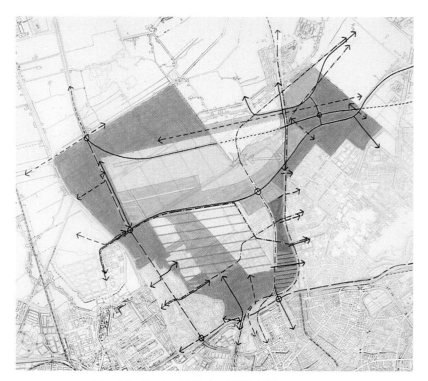

Integral Plan Noordrand Rotterdam (IPNR), 1993.

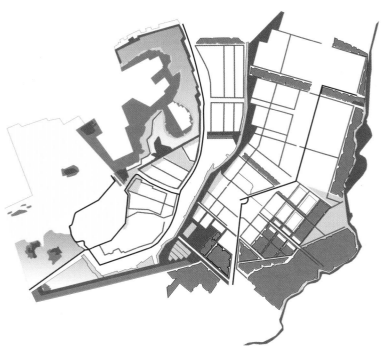

Plan for the green matrix of 2B3, 1995.

matrix. The finely woven nature of this structure allowed the district's neighborhoods to be built with a fairly high degree of density (about 50 dwellings per hectare).

The New Landscape as a Mainstay of Quality

In 'classic' districts, vegetation functions merely to create a more pleasant residential atmosphere: greenery to please the eye or greenery for recreational purposes. In new districts such as IPNR and 2B3, the green matrix has a multi-faceted significance: it is a mainstay of both ecology and infrastructure, it functions as a water balance and as a source of water for greenhouse agriculture, and it plays the role of recreational route. Apparently, realization of uninterrupted green matrices in new districts is possible only when based on such layered implications. Moreover, it is vital for the new green matrix to make use of the existing landscape. With the exception of mud flats on its western border, the area of development covered by the IPNR lacks attractive natural qualities. The plan includes a large landscape element meant to symbolize the identity of the new residential district: a lake, which serves as *the* IPNR orientation point. The lake is important not only because it serves recreational and water-balancing functions for the district; it also plays a role at a higher hierarchical level. It is a crucial link in the (wet) ecological connection between Midden-Delfland and the city. Within the garden cities on Rotterdam's northern periphery, water is an important urban-planning motif. Hillegersberg and Schiebroek have their small lakes and canals. Vlaardingen-Holy has the Vlaardingervaart and Schiedam the Poldervaart (both canals). IPNR's lake is an addition to these. The banks of the lake offer many possibilities for a diversity of densities and living environments. Existing sports-field and allotment-garden complexes in the IPNR's area of development allow for a flexible, long-term approach. To begin with, many of these recreational complexes can continue to serve the new district. In the future, within the framework of open-space functions, such complexes will have plenty of opportunities to be converted into urban areas or to fulfill other recreational functions.

Developing a New Strategy for the Realization of Open-Space Areas

The 2B3 location derives its qualities, at the highest scale, from large green elements on its borders: Rottewig; Berkelse Boog, an offshoot of Midden-Delfland; and the planned 'intermediary' zone of vegetation and water between Bergschenhoek and Rotterdam. The area of development covered by 2B3 is not continuous, such as that of Prinsenland or Rijs en Daal, but composed of a variety of sites scattered here and there. Because of its fragmented composition and the absence of normative and financial 'gifts,' the design of the planned area cannot include, as did Prinsenland and the IPNR, large-scale open-space elements such as lakes and parks distributed throughout the housing areas. Existing elements such as ribbon development, dikes, and canals serve a regulatory function within the location. Just as ribbon development in Prinsenland, these elements have been received with open arms and used to lend identity to the area, an identity complemented by the addition of water in the form of canals. Remaining open-space structure consists of linear elements: utilitarian zones for railroad infrastructure and greenhouse agriculture. The route for the high-speed railroad line runs straight across the planned area. Owing to noise-abatement standards, zones on both sides of the route – at least 2 by 15 meters, with 4-meter-high sound barrier s– are off-limits to housing. This restriction forms a solid basis for a permanent green matrix. These zones provide space for sports and recreational facilities to serve the new district. A comparable 'gift' is born of the need for reservoirs to serve greenhouse agriculture in the area. By combining and connecting reservoirs, a continuous series of lakes is created, and these in turn play an ecological and recreational role at a higher-than-local level. Consequently, elements of greenery that determine the quality of the area are no longer the result of demands made by the new district, but the product of cleverly exploited external claims.

Questions

In former planning situations, it was taken for granted that government was responsible for entire urban districts, down to the last brick: roads, verdure, facilities, and housing. This is no longer true. Most sites currently being developed involve huge sums of money; these are often out-of-the-way locations with soil contaminated by previous land development. Furthermore, vast areas of land have already been bought up by speculators. Long before the first building is realized, therefore, government has invested heavily in preparing the land for new construction and in making it accessible. In comparison with previous expansion areas, governmental funds per dwelling have been reduced, and high starting costs exert even more pressure on the housing budget; extra money for the realization of green areas is virtually nonexistent. The green matrix, along with the infrastructure, falls under the category of collective facilities. Even if it cannot offer full financial support, government should realize at least the essential components of such facilities. Nevertheless, although funds are allocated for infrastructure, the green matrix is still ignored. Thus it will take some clever ruse and a detour or two to acquire funds needed to realize the green matrix desired by all. Examples mentioned here offer several options. The question is where to invest the money: in the internal structure of landscape in districts and neighborhoods, in the regional green matrix outside the districts, or in a combination of the two? Rather than classic urban-expansion projects, such as Prinsenland in Rotterdam, many new-construction sites accommodate housing locations unrelated to other sites, in which more than one municipality is involved, such as 2B3. This site belongs to neither Rotterdam, The Hague, nor Zoetermeer, but to small municipalities between these cities. Therefore, the project involves more than the planned location itself; it must be formulated on a larger, regional scale

as well. When the task at hand crosses boundaries and has a higher-than-local level of importance, municipalities, as a rule, hire outside firms to coordinate and design the project. The green matrix assumes a major role in many of the designs created. Questions to be answered are: what will be preserved and on what scale, and is the private sector prepared to invest in the green matrix as a mainstay of the new housing environment?

Prinsenland

PRINSENPARK
RINGVAARTPLAS
RINGVAARTPLAS NEIGHBORHOOD EAST

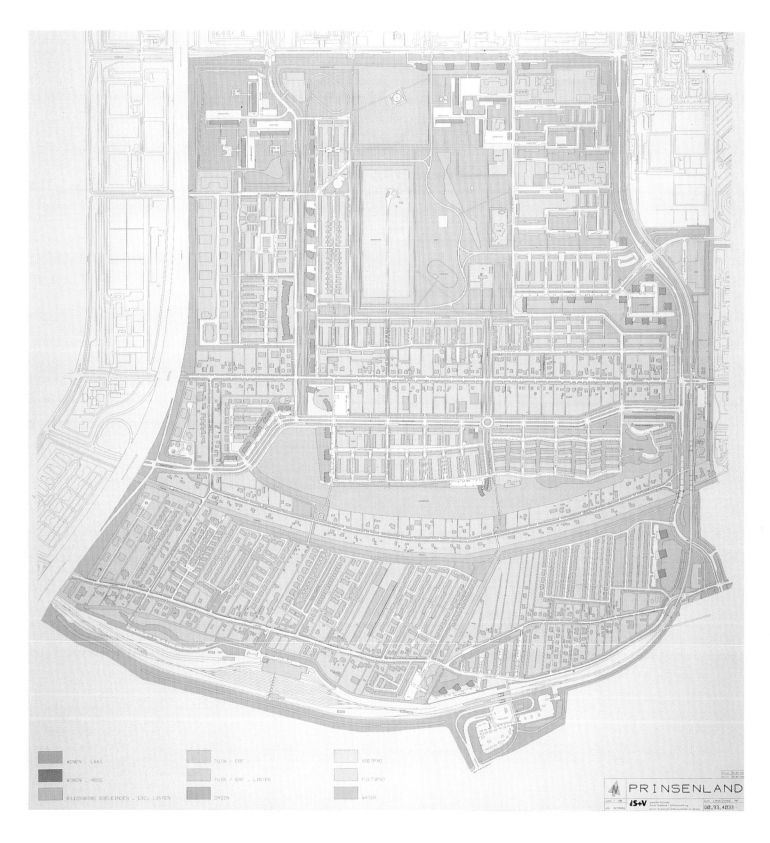

Prinsenland is the most recently developed district in the RoCa area: the area for which the Municipalities of Rotterdam and Capelle aan den IJssel drew up an intermunicipal structure plan for the benefit of urban expansion. Within the boundaries of Rotterdam, the RoCa area covers all districts within the borough of Prins Alexander. Although Prinsenland is

closer to the city center than are the districts of Ommoord, Oosterflank, Zevenkamp, and Het Lage Land, it was developed later. The reason is that land in Prinsenland - a densely built-up greenhouse area - was difficult to acquire. The area was to accommodate 2,000 existing dwellings, to which 5,000 new ones would be added. Besides that very sizable housing program, there was also an elaborate program for open space. To be realized were green facilities for residents of Prinsenland at block, neighborhood, and district levels, as well as extra recreational open space to compensate for the lack of same, according to WKWR standards, in Het Lage Land and Oosterflank. Furthermore, the municipality placed great importance on landscape that was to be converted into a housing area. Originally, Prinsenland was part of a vast area of peat bogs. In the Middle Ages, some of the bogs east of Rotterdam were drained for agrarian use; resulting land division was based on long, narrow parcels called *slagen*. Farms went up along 's-Gravenweg, the backbone of this develop-

ment. Later, in response to an increasing demand for fuel to supply the growing cities, peat was cut from the marshy *slagen*, beginning north of Rotterdam in the vicinity of a road now known as Ringvaartweg. Peat was removed at such a pace that a continuous area of lakes was created. With the exception of Kralingse Lake, these lakes were drained in the nineteenth century and the land, reclaimed and divided into polders, was once more parceled out in *slagen*. Ribbon development appeared along both Ringvaartweg and 's-Gravenweg. Thus as a result of historical developments, the area of Prinsenland was split in two: south of Ringvaartweg, a medieval peatbog landscape divided into *slagen*, and north of Ringvaartweg, a younger landscape marked by reclamation. A difference in elevation between the two measures 4 meters. The reclaimed land consisted of more than meadows and ditches. In order to shorten the traveling distance between Rotterdam and Gouda, a new road, straight as an arrow, was laid across this area: Kralingseweg. Furthermore, a

URBAN EXPANSION AND LANDSCAPE DEVELOPMENT

cemetery was built in the midst of the meadows, on a number of raised *slagen*. This cemetery, Oud Kralingen, is accessed by a small lane perpendicular to Kralingseweg.

In planning the new district, several ground rules concerning the landscape were established: the difference between the two types of landscape – especially the difference in elevation – was to remain recognizable, and historical elements were to be preserved. In addition, the green matrix was to be linked to the area surrounding Prinsenland; proposed were two east-west-oriented green belts, which would connect Kralingse Woods with Scholle Woods in Capelle aan den IJssel. The initial concept behind the structure of open space consisted of the veins of a green belt running through the district, verdure that would include existing ribbon development and the cemetery. Cutting this somewhat amorphous green area in two was the first step in developing the ultimate concept of an urban district that reflects the underlying structure of the landscape. Openness was

a must in keeping the curve of Ringvaartweg visible and in emphasizing the difference in elevation between north and south. This openness was realized by means of a large lake along Ringvaartweg. Residential neighborhoods line the lake, as does a shopping center. The northern section of the district was to include greenery in the form of low-rise housing with private gardens, but the plan for landscape verdure provided no space for these gardens. Therefore, a large park, located close to the existing districts of Het Lage Land and Oosterflank, was projected for this section. The cemetery was incorporated into this park, and additional facilities include a school, swimming pool, and children's farm. Park and lake are linked by north-south-oriented canals. A 25-meter-wide green strip was realized along the Ringvaart Canal. Together these elements form a solid, permanent framework that provides the district with its own identity. Lake and park have become Prinsenland's trademark.

In designing the neighborhoods, a great

deal of attention was given to the so-called 'warp and weft.' Wherever possible and desirable, lines of vision leading to historical ribbon development, lake, or park have been incorporated into the urban-planning subdivision of land. A new road lies between the broad end of the lake and the shopping center: Jacques Dutilhweg. It has assumed the important function of a thoroughfare, formerly held by Kralingseweg. Then, too, remaining ribbon-development routes are not as busy as they were in the past and can now function as routes for slow-moving traffic. Ringvaartweg, therefore, with lake, canal, and green belt, is one of the desired, connective, recreational green zones. The newly realized Prinsenlaan, a northern east-west connection linking Kralingse Woods, the park, and the strip of parkland along Oosterflank, is less continuous.

Because the main urban-planning scheme calls for neighborhoods to be situated around large areas accommodating outdoor recreation, it was possible to add small, normatively required, walkable green facilities to the area of park and lake. Thus the customary dispersion of block, neighborhood, and district verdure has been omitted. It was also possible to divide neighborhoods into economical parcels; Prinsenland's land-use percentage is high. In the strip that divides Ringvaartweg and 's-Gravenweg, a developer subdivided the land on the basis of demands made by municipal departments and of preconditions pertaining to exploitation and structure of the landscape. Land between Ringvaartweg and 's-Gravenweg has been raised only partially. The original ditches have been preserved where possible, and the directions taken by roads in this area echo historical patterns of land division. Low-density, low-rise housing realized here consists of about 20 dwellings per hectare. The urban-planning scheme for the area north of Ringvaartweg calls for high-density, compact neighborhoods - an average of 55 dwellings per hectare - with their own identity, to be determined largely by the architecture of the housing. For the most part, the architects designed large clusters, some of which include 200 units. In so doing, they worked according to preconditions drawn up by municipal planners and open-space designers. The spatial image of the neighborhoods is determined by the composition of the streets. Each street had its own requirements: front gardens, no front gardens; large front gardens, small front gardens; symmetrical layout, asymmetrical layout; and so forth. Parking on the streets was solved in various ways. Few trees line the residential streets. A substantial number, however, have been planted along canals and in green strips. The most important paving materials used in laying streets were gray concrete slabs, gray concrete curbs, and gray concrete bricks. This aesthetic and financial restraint made it possible to particularize public space at locations such as the shopping center, where a high level of quality was desired. Thus the strategy involving a realization of surplus spatial value through a concentration of resources was applied at the level of the structure plan as well as that of project plans.

Prinsenpark

Submunicipality • PRINS ALEXANDER

Designer • BUREAU B + B, MICHAEL VAN GESSEL; dS+V, AD KOOLEN

Artist • FRANS DE WIT

Type of plan • PARK

Qualitative level • STANDARD-PLUS/SELECT

Management level • INTENSIVE/EXTENSIVE

Surface area • 350.500 m²

Date planning began • 1985

Date of completion • 1994 - 1995

Apportionment fund • F 33.000.000,-

Layout costs • F 103,-/m²

Prinsenpark was developed together with the urban plan for Prinsenland. Such simultaneous development is exceptional. As a result, plan development for the park has not only covered a long period of time but has also influenced the urban-planning concept of the district. Originally, the intention was to preserve existing meadowlands in this part of Prinsenland and to provide them with an unpretentious layout geared to the informal character of a large number of backyards. Ultimately, this approach was abandoned. The park is conceived as an urban element filled with greenery. Such an exceptional feature of the city must be open to the public and must be made extra attractive. Therefore, the park is bordered by streets for motorized traffic, and facades of surrounding buildings face its verdure. The design of the park is highly architectonic.

Owing to the distinct design and to the use of characteristic species of trees and shrubs, each section of the park has its own ambience and calls for a specific form of use. A double row of cherry trees on a gravel surface lines the periphery of the park. This row creates a definite border and offers a walk around the park with a view of the lower, central area. Within the austere framework of trees lies Oud Kralingen Cemetery, existing facili-

ties, and new elements - hill and arena - which form separate components of a spatial composition. Urban additions pay no heed to the original structure of the landscape, but in the old cemetery, the grass, and the ditches, reclamation operations resound as an echo from the past. On Prinsenlaan, an existing woodland spot has made way for a square lake. The objective here is to offer a view of the surroundings and a point of orientation to those passing the park on the Prinsenlaan side. Passersby are to be attracted by a special element in the lake. Original plans projected a magnolia garden here; finally, however, the decision was made to place a sculpture here, which will symbolize what is alleged to be the lowest spot in the Netherlands.

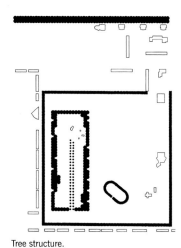

Tree structure.

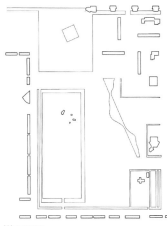

Waterways.

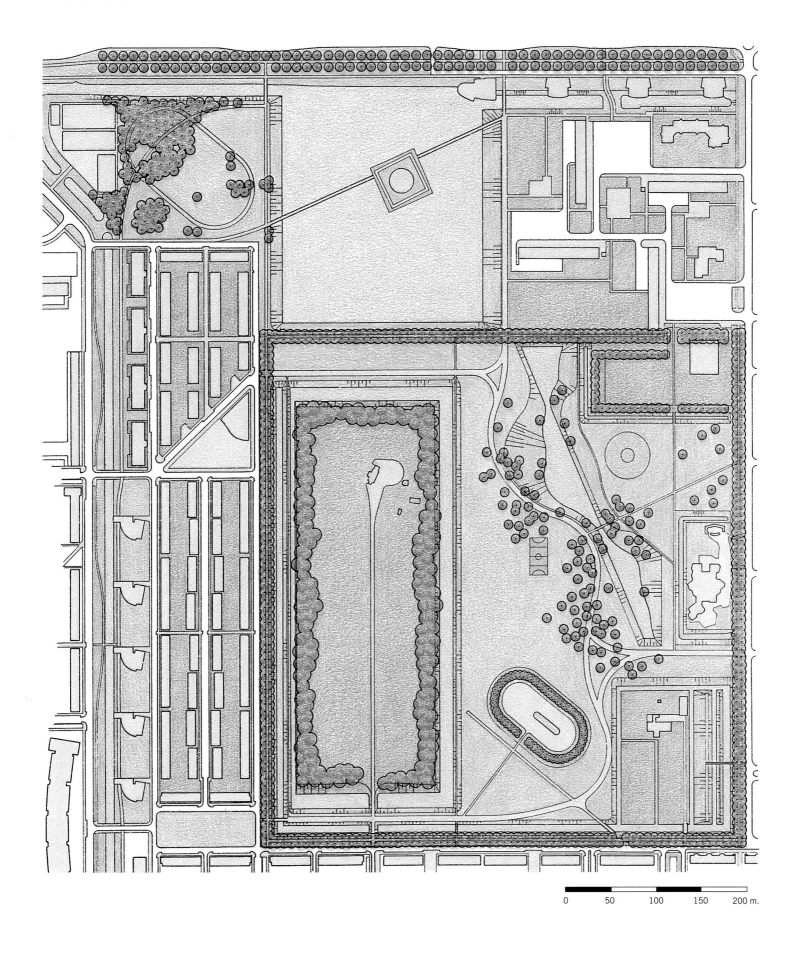

URBAN EXPANSION AND LANDSCAPE DEVELOPMENT

0   50   100   150   200 m.

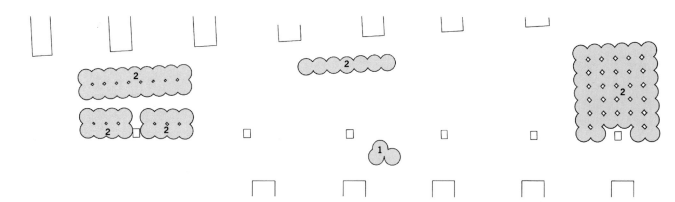

The remaining three fields are seeded with grass. At a spot between neighborhoods, where a transverse route crosses the park, a group of chestnut trees has been planted. The limited budget has resulted in highly austere detailing. Unfortunately, a lack of funds can also be blamed for the omission of lighting above the doors of stopcock houses along the pedestrian route.

Technical data

Because the masonry of brick walls composing the filter basins was in poor condition, it had to be repaired before filling the basins.

Ashlar nosing, most of which had disappeared, was replaced by concrete slabs, which were tooled in an attempt to reproduce the original image.

To create a natural water balance in the basins, holes bored in the floor were filled with gravel. The existing layer of filtration sand was covered with another layer of gravel, and this was topped with a drainage cloth. The design of the park also calls for certain basins to be filled with sand or ground.

DESIGNING A CITY-RIVER RELATIONSHIP

Dokhavenpark

Submunicipality • CHARLOIS
Designer • dS+V, PAUL ACHTERBERG
Artist • BERNARD OLSTHOORN, JAN VAN IJZENDOORN

Type of plan • PARK
Qualitative level • STANDARD +
Management level • INTENSIVE
Surface area • 40.000 m²
Date planning began • 1984
Date of completion • 1988 - 1989

Apportionment fund • F 3.250.000,-
Layout costs • F 81,-/ m²

In 1976 the municipality decided to use the Dokhaven site, outside the dikes, as an overspill area for the adjacent urban-renewal district of Charlois. An elongated, curved, angular apartment building of varying heights was projected for Charloisse Hoofd; the front of the structure faces the Maas Tunnel Building. Gallery apartments designed for the other side of Dokhaven form a long, straight wall perpendicular to the river. It was not until after these plans had been developed that the decision was made to build a new water-purification plant in the Dokhaven area as well. Such a step could

be taken only by locating the installation as a sort of 'box' deep within the harbor basin and using its roof as a park. The water-purification box is at right angles to the river; after the harbor area around the plant was filled in, there remained a triangular building site. This site accommodates urban villas and row housing. Finally, development on the west side of the newly created riverfront ends with a tall apartment tower. In its totality, the urban plan has become a composition consisting of various types of subdivision. Development here makes it difficult to traverse the area without getting lost. Its location, on a gentle outer bend of the river, provides riverside views of both banks of the Maas, but amid the development, the proximity of the river goes unnoticed.
Because the park is a centrally located area of open space and is linked to the

spaciousness of the river, it must be a consolidating hub for the district and a spot that lends distinction to the Dokhaven site. In designing the park, an attempt was made to draw as much of the riverscape experience into the area as possible. Furthermore, the industrial character of the purification plant beneath the park became a main theme in the design. The flat, graphic layout of the park resembles the parterre of a French baroque garden. Lines within its orthogonal composition are determined by the purification plant. The contours of the roof are visible on the surface in the form of concrete, earth-retaining elements and brick walls. The spatial effect of the low retaining walls is impressive, especially when the sun casts long shadows. The treatment of the roof as a container has a dual effect: the layer of earth on top of the concrete experiences very

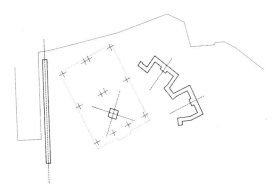

Original situation: lack of coherence.

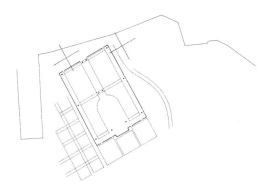

Main modification: introduction of an orthogonal system.

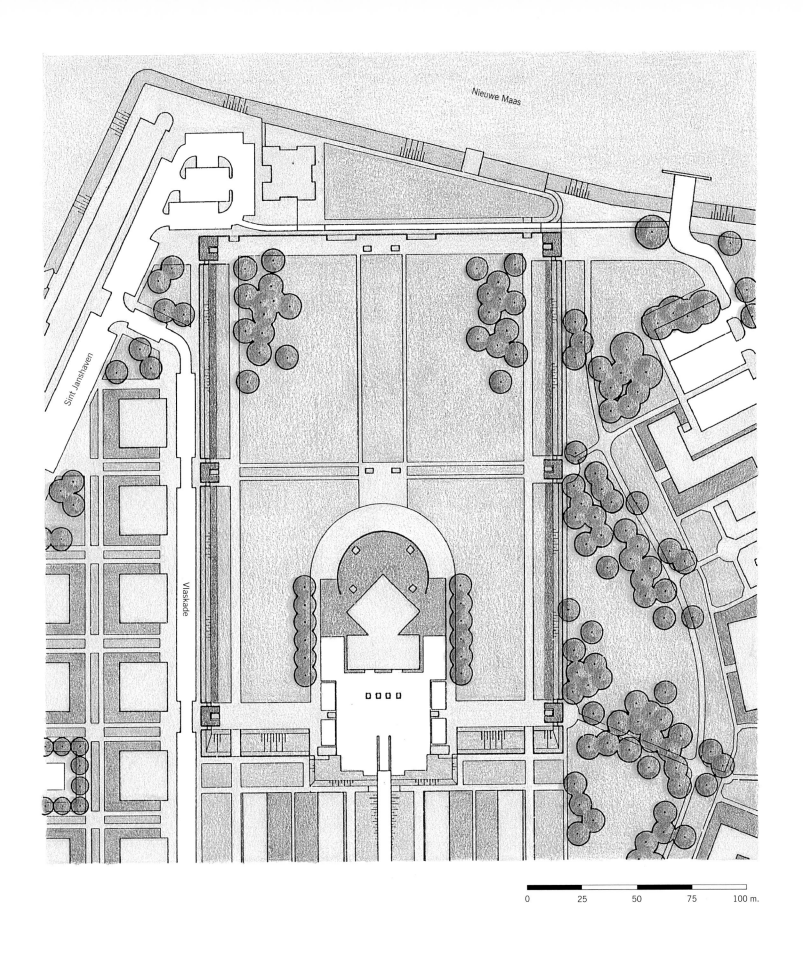

Nieuwe Maas

Sint Janshaven

Vlaskade

0   25   50   75   100 m.

little subsidence, a fact that does not apply to the surrounding surface.

The square service building atop the purification plant dominates the park area, but, being diagonally positioned, it lacks a sense of association with the rectangle of the roof. Consequently, the building is included within a basal area of grass that flows toward the open riverfront like a vast carpet. To reinforce the perception of depth as the eye focuses on the river, this area is separated spatially from areas on either side. Several groups of trees planted here lessen the formality of this austere expanse, which is reminiscent of historical public meadows once found in Rotterdam. In addition to the service building, the underground complex also calls attention to itself through emergency exits in the middle of the roof and along the periphery. They are connected by a system of dual path-

ways, which creates rhythm and a perspective effect. Further references to the industrial character of the site are fences designed especially for the park. Their cruciformity calls to mind details of fences found in industrial buildings and nineteenth-century fortifications. The space between the purification plant and housing on Charloisse Hoofd has a more introverted and informal character. This area has been planted with individual groups of gray poplars and also accommodates a sunken playground for children.

Technical data

The level of the roof of the purification plant corresponds to the ground level of its surroundings (4.00 m above Amsterdam ordnance datum). A 1.00-meter layer of earth atop the roof is contained by 1.00-meter-high, brick or concrete retaining walls at the edge of the roof and

by specially designed 0.50-meter-high, earth-retaining elements attached to the edge of the roof.

In determining the composition of this layer of soil, those involved thought in terms of what a tree requires from its habitat: sufficient light, moisture, and nutrients, as well as solid anchorage. When a tree gets the chance to spread its roots 0.50 m or deeper and to develop well horizontally, the danger that it will fall on a windy day is slight. Therefore, ground-water level must be at least 0.50 m below ground level. The soil used here ranges from a humuslike, heavy loam to a light clay, with a thickness varying from 0.80 m to 1.10 m and a lutum content between 17.5 and 35.0 per thousand. A 0.30-meter-thick layer of coarse sand beneath the clay layer accommodates a drainage system. A rapid and uninterrupted removal of water prevents unde-

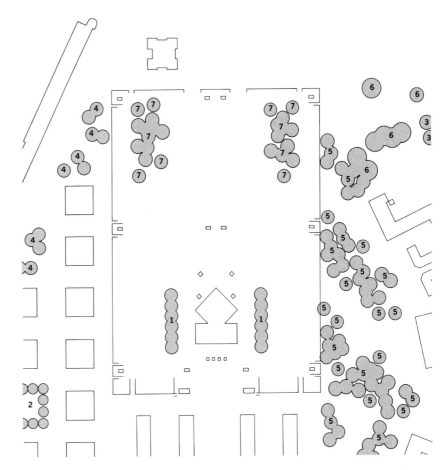

Trees Dokhavenpark

1. Alnus incana • Grey alder
2. Alnus spaethii • Alder
3. Fraxinus exelsior • Ash
4. Populus alba • White poplar
5. Populus canescens 'Limbricht' • Poplar
6. Populus euramericana • Poplar
7. Ulmus hollandica 'Groeneveld' • Elm

sired fluctuations in the ground-water level and thus assures an optimal soil profile for the growth of healthy roots. From the outset, the weight of sand, clay, trees and other vegetation, architectonic facilities, ground water, and so forth was taken into consideration by those designing the construction of the roof.

The park is intensively managed. Nevertheless, agreements have been made with the maintenance staff about relations between areas of the park requiring intensive and extensive maintenance. Hedges are trimmed twice a year, and soft edges (such as tree surrounds) are clipped two to three times a year. Paths consist of asphalt with a porous layer covered with white pearl gravel. Hard edges are tidied five times annually. The linear design favors the use of a new machine to maintain path borders. This machine cuts the edges, cleanly burns the adjoining meter of land, and vacuums up the refuse.

DESIGNING A CITY-RIVER RELATIONSHIP

'Do-it-yourself marts have far too much influence on the quality of open space'

An interview with Hans Kranenburg, project manager of Bouwfonds Woningbouw (Building Fund for Housing) in Hoevelaken

'THERE IS LITTLE COMPARISON BETWEEN THE WAY in which major urban-expansion projects are organized today and the way in which they were organized several years ago. According to the traditional method, the municipality involved initiated the formulation of a plan and took responsibility for highways, streets, watercourses, and public utilities. Subsequently, developers, contractors, and real-estate agents – selected for the most part on the basis of unfathomable criteria– were given the opportunity to build housing and offer it for sale. This process still occurs in the same way at certain places, but in many other cases, the municipality is no longer the most important purchaser of agricultural areas for housing sites. Larger organizations, such as the Bouwfonds, are often the first in line to acquire property. Consequently, negotiations with the municipality begin at a much earlier stage. The purchasing process depends greatly on what the central and provincial governments reveal about their policies on the direction to be taken by urbanization, both in the short term and over a longer period of time. Therefore, we follow the physical-planning policy very closely and participate in policy discussion as well.

We've been building housing in the Netherlands for 50 years, but owing to changes in context, we operate more often than we used to in the area of what might be called site engineering. From the beginning of the plan-development process, we try, together with the municipality, to find a common developmental denominator and to put it into a contract. Having done so, we're in a position to be the intermediary between municipal administrators, who dictate the conditions, and builders and housing administrators, who are in charge of implementation. We stay right on top of things during the entire building process in order to see that everything gets done according to the agreements made. Being an intermediary means that we're constantly prepared to assess whether things are going as planned. The efficiency of the development and the spatial quality both benefit from this approach.

The housing market is also subject to shifts. At the moment, most of what we realize are free-sector, owner-occupied dwellings. For this reason, we try to analyze and understand what people want in housing and to find a contemporary form in which to express those desires. It's tempting simply to build dwellings with a through lounge and pitched roof, because that's where the demand lies. In my eyes, such housing provides insufficient ensemble quality and no districts and neighborhoods with a strong identity. In recent years it's chiefly the municipalities who are looking for the integration of environmental-protection features in the building industry. And that's another aspect that can help in producing special types of housing. In my experience with the development of Ecolonia in Alphen aan de Rijn, a district in which principles of durability set the tone, I learned that after awhile, certain occupants of environmentally friendly dwellings will start fiddling with the facilities. The "gray-water circuit" no longer functions well, and the space taken up by solar boilers and such is needed for other things. Only the largest dwellings still satisfy gradually changing, individual housing demands, because those are the ones offering the most flexibility. I've come to the conclusion that housing, in all its facets, is so much more - and should be - than just keeping down the cost of heating and not staying in the shower too long. And the bigger the site, the more difficult it is to impose such principles on everyone. A residential district with 10,000 idealists simply doesn't exist. In the urban-expansion project that I'm working on now, the district of Nieuwland next to Amersfoort, we've decided to raise the durability to the district level. To lend expression to other, more spatial objectives, we call it the Garden City of Nieuwland.

In the plan for Nieuwland, which we commissioned Bureau Wissing to draw up for us, various limitations of the site were cleverly converted into special features. For example, one major disadvantage was the location next to a busy highway at the edge of the city. Noise pollution was reduced by erecting a wall around the district, which also gives a sense of security to the housing environment. Part of the wall will be realized by positioning housing up against it, thus creating a special type of housing. The top surface of the wall will double as a promenade, so that soon you can view the whole district and the landscape beyond from a height of several meters. Sand for the wall was taken from the site, a step that allowed for the realization of good water control; the plan includes storage and purification of water for the district. The centrally located district park is a kind of water accumulator: a facility that guarantees balanced water control for the district, also in extremely wet or dry periods. Thus I see Nieuwland as an example of urban expansion in which environmental goals are realized in public open space. At the individual level, each household can contribute in its own way, as desired.

The entire plan for the design of public open space is based on achieving large, clear-cut lines. In order to simplify management, we want to avoid vegetation that needs mowing and pruning, and for this reason, we've decided to sell the land per square meter instead of in complete parcels. Within limits, homeowners can determine the shape of their property themselves and gear the architecture to those dimensions. In this way, there will be few leftover pieces of land, since most people enjoy having large gardens. To encourage the creation of a unified streetscape, despite this increase in freedom of choice, and to prevent the quality of your own house being diminished by your neighbor's decisions, we decided to limit greenery separating private gardens from public domain to one species only. At the moment residents move in, this greenery will have been planted on the side facing the street. My experience with other newly built districts has taught me that do-it-yourself marts have far too much influence on the quality of open space. By making a preinvestment in private open space, we're able to limit that influence to some extent.

When buying a home in Nieuwland, each resident receives a kind of manual, which explains the intention behind the physical layout of the district and the role of the various elements in it. The manual contains suggestions for creating partitions between gardens, as well as a code of behavior and agreements on the organization of neighborhood and district management in the areas of waste disposal, for instance, and maintenance of public space. I imagine that later, when property changes hands, such information will be distributed by neighborhood community centers. In this way, residents' attention will continue to be directed to communal conditions for spatial quality.'

Plan for the residential district of Nieuwland (Amersfoort) by Bureau Wissing (consultancy on urban planning and spatial design), 1995.

'For me, the tension between topography and program is the essence of the profession'

An interview with Frits Palmboom, urban planner and member of the urban-planning consultancy Palmboom and Van den Bout in Rotterdam

'THERE EXISTS A VAGUELY DEFINED IDEA that shifts in clientage explicitly affect the quality of residential districts. Programmatically and procedurally, this is indeed an issue. Shifts appear in the distribution of responsibility and risk, but this doesn't lead directly to an intrinsically different design problem. A lot depends on the question of whether or not the client will remain involved in the use and management of the neighborhoods for an extended period of time. Generally speaking, I sense a recent increase in the amount of attention paid to the design of open space, but this isn't coming exclusively from municipal departments, or from developers or real-estate agents. I notice in my contacts with marketing people that they underline the importance of a well-designed housing environment. It's true that many of them are thinking of a traditional housing image and are referring, in general, to neighborhoods from the 1930s, but even so, the demand exists. In a few cases, such as in the plan for Ypenburg, those involved have been receptive to maintaining relations between the residential district and the greater surroundings – call it spatial anchorage. I see an evolving clientage within the sphere of housing environment and open space. It's up to urban planning to nurture this evolution. The relationship between private and public, along with a search for balance between the two in the urban plan, is also shifting. This has a sociocultural background. Culture, which places great emphasis on collectivity, as expressed in the Siedlung concept - the district idea in its social-democratic or corporatist version - is being replaced by something else. Kiefhoek and Vreewijk were based on an explicit collectivity. The housing culture has experienced an extreme change. It's focusing more and more on variation and multiformity, on individuality. There exists today a strange tension between privacy and exhibitionism. The home is simultaneously a personal domain and a display case. The sense of community is disappearing. This sense was once a very powerful structural motif in our profession, but now it's a spent cartridge. This is one of the reasons why I've come to see landscape as a foundation. Landscape possesses different kinds of structural and design motifs, which are bound to yield something spatially interesting.

I go to manipulated landscape, stripped of its sentimental connotations, for advice. In both a physical and economic sense, individuals are becoming less and less tied to the phenomenon of the city as a place with an identity. We live in built-up conurbations, certainly in the western part of our country. In the Ypenburg expansion area, an unequivocal orientation toward church towers or market squares is nowhere to be found. In order to counterbalance the fragmentary battle for prestige being fought by the various participating municipalities, I've tried to find an answer in the hydrologic and traffic-engineering organization of the landscape. As a planner, this is where my moral principles begin and end. I find it challenging, gratifying, and inspirational just to give shape to the complexity of society and to the paradoxes it holds. It would be going too far to say that the objective of the urban plan is to have people relate to their origins. The landscape simply forms – as do the building program and the financial-economic criteria – a foundation for the design process. Another clearly visible phenomenon is a shift in relationships between disciplines in the field of spatial design. Contrary to what some people claim, I think that urban planning and landscape architecture are still autonomous professions. The two have a close disciplinary kinship and overlap to some extent when it comes to the object of design. But there's a big difference in roles and responsibilities. As planner, you relate indirectly to building and, along with that, to architecture. As an urban planner, I'm more tuned in to architecture than are most landscape architects. They have an affinity for growth and for paving, for the actual creation of the basal area. They also prepare for a form of building, but it's related to the materialization of open space, both public and private. I find the collaboration between disciplines very inspirational, because it broadens my own affinity. This collaboration should be highly intense, without causing the participants to resemble each other.

I wouldn't like to see the role of urban planner limited to that of physical programmer. For me, the tension between topography and program is the essence of the profession. Within this field of tension, the planner uses the spatial design as an instrument. An architectonic and compositional dimension is inextricably bound to this process. There's a rediscovery of the spatial program as a design motif. The program – as the power that provides the city with shape and significance – is very important. But this develops through a great many channels and not only in the domain of the urban planner. Before you know it, this preoccupation with the program is translated into a kind of neo-functionalism, and the impact of the spatial design is disregarded.

Willem-Jan Neutelings's manifesto on the carpet metropolis is a borderline case, in my opinion. The narrative is brilliant; suspense builds as the author looks at the way in which people move through space and at what they use to get their bearings. He shows how, in our perception, old topographical relationships are being replaced by new ones. He's created very clever metaphors to explain such things. At the same time, I don't believe that current spatial points of departure, such as city streets and tree-lined avenues, are becoming completely irrelevant. On the contrary, I find it highly fascinating that age-old and ultramodern patterns blend together, overlap, and still continue to go on functioning. Recognizing this complexity and imbuing it with new meaning in a plan is, I feel, my professional responsibility. Urban planning is more often "adding to" than "replacing." I'd like to question Neutelings about the composition of the carpet as a problem of spatial design. Spatial redesign of the topography to allow for the accommodation of new programs is one of the specific tasks of the urban planner.'

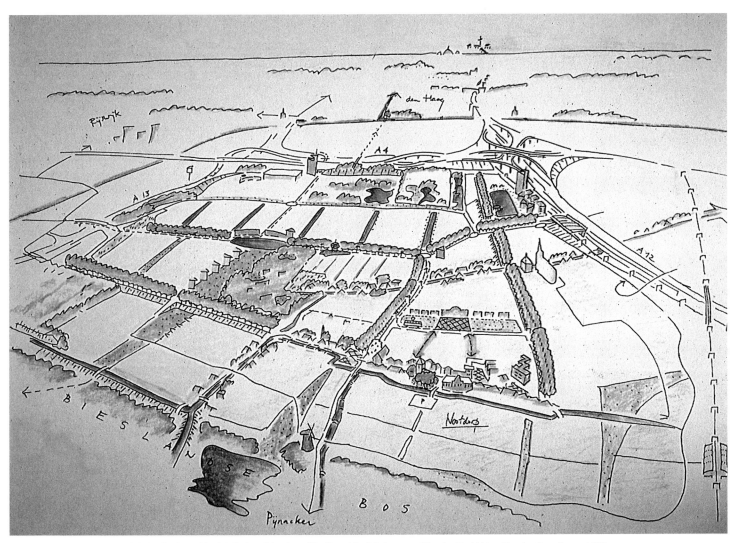

Aerial plan for the residential district of Ypenburg (The Hague) by Palmboom and Van den Bout Urban Planning Consultancy, 1995.

The City Center and Subcentral Areas

The Creation of Inner-City Open Space

Postwar reconstruction of Rotterdam's city center has been completed. After 50 years, the inner city once more radiates a natural vitality. Spots in which to recreate, to shop, to stroll, and to be entertained are accommodated in easily recognized areas. This situation is a result of the fusion between special functions and surrounding areas of open space.

The center of Rotterdam has known a turbulent history. Even before the bombardment, the old City Triangle had been rejected. This historical center around Binnenrotte was dominated by the railroad viaduct and housing areas of little distinction. It was a cramped and claustrophobic inner city. Apart from the main marketplace, the Grotemarkt, located

on a filled-in section of old harbor basins, there was no other square or public place that could be called the heart of the city. Rotterdam, wanting to shed the image of ugly provincial town, made several attempts to clean up the inner city. Ultimately, these led to the transformation of Coolsingel, on the periphery of the City Triangle, into a distinguished boulevard. First the red-light district was replaced by a new city hall, which was followed later by the main post office, the Bijenkorf Department Store, and the stock exchange.

After the war, a tremendous opportunity presented itself to follow in the direction already begun: the desire for a new city center, worthy of a port city, could be fulfilled. This center provided space for office buildings, retail facilities, and cultural accommodations. Such functions were embedded within a precisely defined system of open space, which included inner-city courtyards, shopping streets, delivery roads, weekly markets, and a theater square. The organization of these open-space areas was geared wherever possible to a specific function. The best-known example is, without a doubt, Lijnbaan, where open space is entirely devoted to urban residents out shopping or taking a stroll.

Special attention was given to the disposition of Coolsingel. By forcing a direct breakthrough to Leuvehaven and the Maas, a new relationship was created between city and river. The continuation of Coolsingel provided the new city center with a 'window to the river.' The significance of this distinctive boulevard was reinforced by the construction of the new Bijenkorf and other department stores. Furthermore, Coolsingel grew into the open-space area in which Feyenoord celebrates major victories, demonstrations are held, and the annual marathon begins and ends.

Current Areas of Operation

The task currently facing the urban center is no longer the (re)construction of a destroyed inner city but the transformation of the existing city. The inner city needs to be constantly adapted to the continuously changing urban reality it must assimilate. Open space can play a crucial organizational role in strategies that include an uncertain future to be faced. Various features of the inner city can be articulated within open space. At the same time, it is this very space in which everyday reality – sometimes pleasant, sometimes shocking – is inevitably present. Open space can underline the importance of a spot, such as Coolsingel does. Sometimes it is an essential component of an area, as in the case of Lijnbaan. And at times it even functions as an urban motor, as does Binnenrotte. In this way, ambitions are defined and activities generated.

Open space in the inner city is highly subject to change. The attractiveness of today's inner city is determined by opportunities for personal encounters and the exchange of ideas; it is born of a high density of cultural activities, amusement, and recreation. More than ever, open space around buildings, the design of which includes programs for its use, forms a specific kind of public domain.

On the one hand, this situation leads to a certain degree of open-space privatization. This tendency is manifested in various ways, ranging from the occupation of public space by sidewalk cafés, retail displays, market stands, and the extensive division of public domain to accommodate various streams of traffic to the – sometimes physically present – supervision and surveillance of parks and shopping streets. On the other hand, a contrasting tendency is also apparent: the urbanization or collectivization of private domain. Private and semipublic areas are increasingly being colonized by various urban groups. Such collective areas, such as shopping centers, cultural organizations, recreational attractions, department stores, public transportation facilities,

hotels, cafés, and restaurants, are becoming a more and more important playing field for everyday urban life. They assimilate some of the activities formerly accommodated by open space. Personal encounters and exchanges now take place much more often in the Bijenkorf, McDonald's, or the lobby of the Doelen than on the street.

Territorial shifts reflect the disappearance of a coherent urban community. Contemporary urban society is composed of a highly diverse scale of urban communities, groups of people who make use of and live in the urban territory. One individual can be a member of many different groups. The urban territory has experienced extensive subdivision into various domains, each of which is dominated by a specific urban community and organized according to its particular norms and rules of play.

A number of recent open-space projects in the city center have entered into a dialogue with this current inner-city reality, because each is defined as an inextricable element of open space *and* as the high point of a public domain.

One Multifaceted Inner City

Rotterdam's inner city is characterized by four distinct areas: the Park Triangle, the Centrumruit (area around the Lijnbaan), the City Triangle, and the Kop van Zuid. Together they form one multifaceted inner city on opposite sides of the river. They are related to one another by three dominant structures that span the river: the cultural route, which extends from Central Station to Wilhelmina Pier; the city axis, which extends from Hofplein to Rijnhaven; and the railroad tunnel route, which uses the strip on which the railroad viaduct was once located to breathe new life into the historic setting accommodating the Church of St. Laurens, Binnenrotte, Oudehaven, and, in Rotterdam South, the Entrepôt area. The specific characters of these areas can be reinforced by focusing on the self-evident theme attached to each. The realization of strategic projects, each of which grants a major role to open space, allows area-related themes to prove their worth, time after time. Rotterdam's most important open-space area is the river. Ever since port activities were moved out of the city, the river's significance for the city center has been undergoing a radical change. Defining this new significance and redesigning the riverbanks represents a translation of the ambition 'city center on the river.' Space has become available for new functions. Quays along river and harbors compose attractive urban-recreational fabric, a highlight of which is the Boompjes. Open space has been adapted to accommodate short-term activities along and on the waterfront. Museumpark provides the theme of the Park Triangle, 'culture and recreation,' with an obvious midpoint. The special significance of this park is expressed in the impressive series of collective cultural programs that it assembles and combines. Furthermore, Museumpark, in its role as open-air podium for nonpermanent cultural activities, forms the active center of this public domain.

The City Triangle can be characterized by the theme 'the

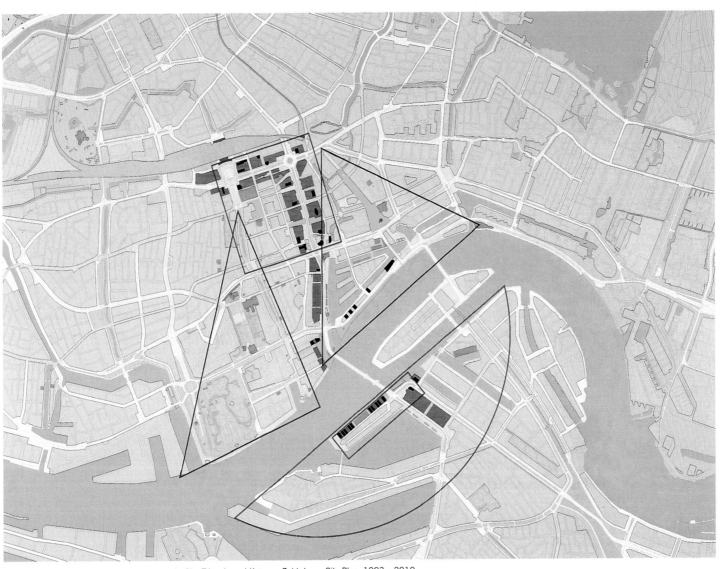

Park Triangle, Centrumruit, City Triangle and Kop van Zuid: Inner-City Plan, 1993 – 2010.

THE CREATION OF INNER-CITY OPEN SPACE

Binnenrotte.

uncommon commonplace of existence.' This theme refers to the vast amount of public interest focused, in particular, on phenomena such as the marketplace, library, Church of St. Laurens, and Oudehaven. Binnenrotte, the central area of the City Triangle, derives its power and naturalness from these collective programs, which it organizes as 'forums.' With the realization of Binnenrotte, a framework of reference was drawn up for the surrounding area, which stands on the threshold of an inescapable process of transformation.

The Centrumruit was given the theme 'shopping and entertainment.' The plan for Schouwburgplein (Theater Square) fills an obvious need for open space in the most densely developed part of the city center. It defines a podium available for intensive use. At the same time, the square will be the open-air lobby of the entertainment sector: the Doelen, the theater, and the new cinema complex.

Beursplein (Stock Exchange Square), the new heart of the central shopping apparatus, perhaps goes the farthest in consolidating collective areas and open space into public domain. Here public space is inextricably linked to the collective – namely, commercial – domain. Open space within this complex functions, first and foremost, as an access and circulation machine but is, in addition, able to organize meaningful encounters between and within various layers and spaces of the composition.

Museumpark.

Boompjes.

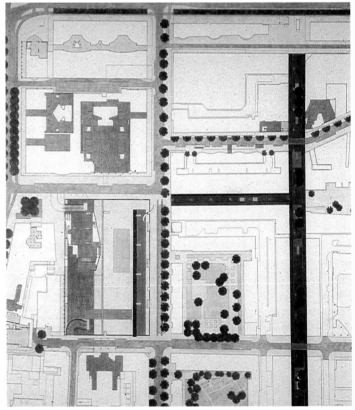

Centrumruit.

The Importance of Urban Open Space

Through the development of specific scenarios for areas
with special features, the reality of the inner city can be
faced with optimism. Open space plays a crucial organizational role within such strategies by placing itself in the
maelstrom of a constantly changing use of the inner city.
Within this situation, the primary significance of open space
lies in its circulative function. It connects and accesses the
vast concentration of inner-city programs and offers space to
a highly intensive network of routes. Considering the specific character of the inner city, most of these routes serve
very slow-moving traffic, such as pedestrians.

Of at least equal importance, however, is the potential of
open space to create measured pauses that relate to specific
conditions. These are disruptive moments in which the
various characteristics of the inner city can be organized and
articulated. They are also moments in which open space can
lock into the collective domain, allowing the identities of
both territories to reinforce each other.

The constant re-creation of inner-city open space makes it
possible to produce a precisely defined system of open areas
that can assimilate existing reality. This network can accommodate the development of specific areas of public domain -
composed of collective areas and open space – which can be
appropriated and used by various urban groups at various
times. Inner-city open space is no longer the place in which
the public interest is self-evident. It is a zone of introduction, a place in which extremes of urban reality can come
together and in which differences can be celebrated.

At times, open space is a component of a complex building;
an example is Beursplein, where open space is a public roof
garden, a mall, and a metro station. At other times, open
space is connected to the landscape, such as along the
Boompjes, where the river is part of an 'urban theater.' The
diversity is extreme; the significance of open space in the
city can no longer be reduced to a common denominator.

Beursplein.

THE CREATION OF INNER-CITY OPEN SPACE

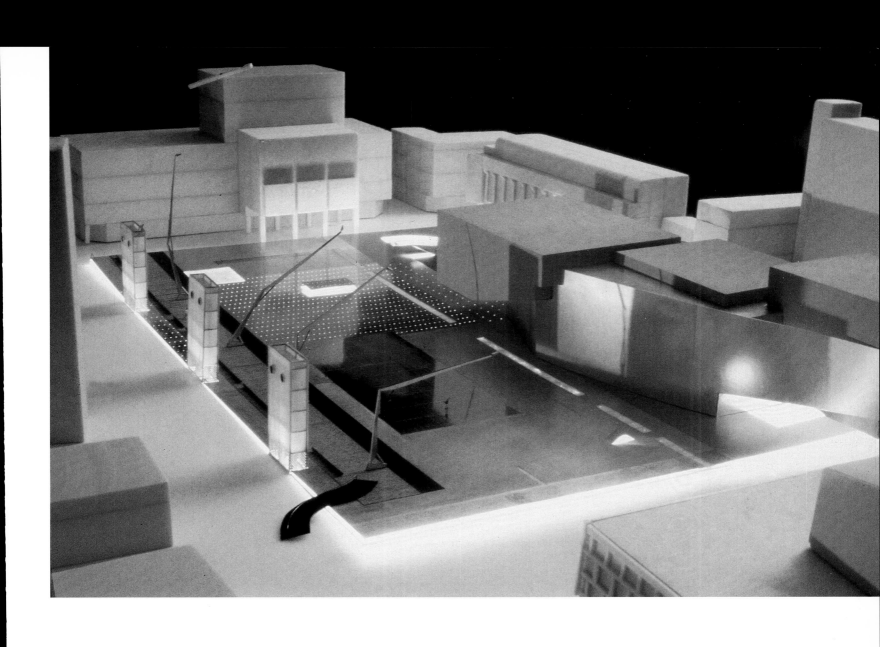

THE CREATION OF INNER-CITY OPEN SPACE

Binnenrotte

Borough • CITY-CENTER

Designer • WEST 8 LANDSCAPE ARCHITECTS, ADRIAAN GEUZE

Type of plan • SQUARE

Qualitative level • EXCLUSIVE

Management level • REPRESENTATIVE

Surface area • 45.500 m²

Date planning began • 1991

Date of completion • 1994 - 1995

Apportionment fund • F 1.200.000,-

Exploitation City-Center • F 2.500.000,-

General Fund • F 100.000,-

Nonmunicipal financing • F 3.000.000,-

BSR-Fund • F 1.840.000,-

Layout costs • F 190,-/m²

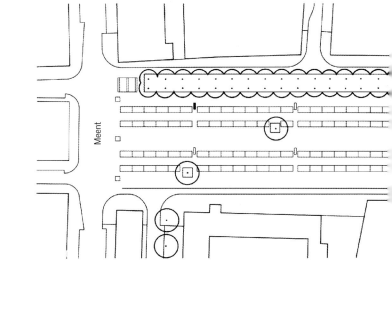

During recent decades the center of Rotterdam has seen a strong increase in density. Excess room around traffic circles and along highways has been utilized, bit by bit, for new housing and office buildings. The replacement of the elevated railroad in the inner city and the railroad bridge over the Maas by a tunnel (1993) has resulted, however, in a large, new area of open space in the inner city: Binnenrotte. Originally, urban plans for the Binnenrotte zone were characterized entirely by the idea of density. The municipality intended to restructure the linear space in such a way that a series of squares would be created: a square next to shopping street de Meent, a square adjacent to the Church of St. Laurens, a square in front of the library, and a square accompanying Blaak Railroad Station. A small shopping arcade, which would lend access to the new underground station, was to serve as a final chapter to the structure of this new development.

Later, a different view of Binnenrotte emerged. The Binnenrotte area is not simply a gap in the urban fabric; it reflects the history of Rotterdam. The Rotte once flowed here. The dimensions of the river and its quays are palpably present within the nearly 600-meter-long and 75-meter-wide zone. All the urban developments that followed are also perceptible. Seen from this standpoint, the multiplicity of rather arbitrarily constructed buildings found within Binnenrotte is not a negative aspect of the area. When the zone is compared to a classical forum, it is even feasible to imagine more buildings being erected here in the future. In addition to the plan to preserve Binnenrotte in its

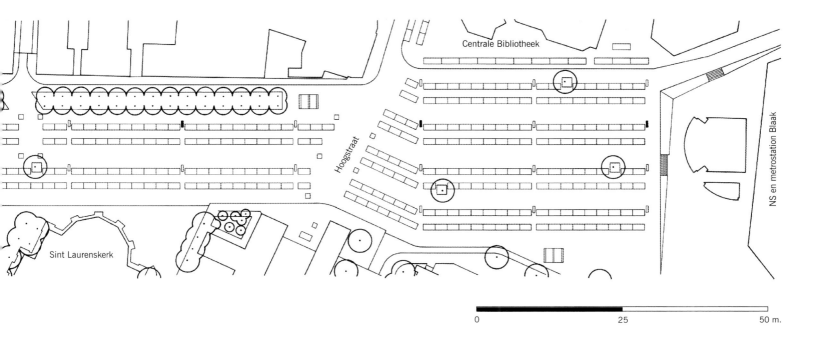

entirety, a plan emerged to re-create the marketplace, which was located next to and under the railroad viaduct before the tunnel was built. With its more than 500 stands, the Rotterdam market is Europe's largest daytime market. Twice a week, when stands are set up and merchandise arrives at the marketplace, an enormous hustle and bustle of activity is unleashed. This activity reaches a high point during the course of the day and ebbs away as stands are dismantled and the process of cleaning up begins. For Binnenrotte, which has no shops and few establishments representing the hospitality industry, the return of the marketplace is accompanied by a rhythmic flux of activity and cessation. Although this large area could also be used for the organization of public events, its market function precludes events of any length.

The marketplace is a determining factor in the identification of Binnenrotte; consequently, its identifying characteristics are expressed in the new organization of the area. For an area so often vacant and of which highly functional demands are made to satisfy the needs of the market, the quality of its surface is crucial. Funds available within a standard budget were used to develop a special, large-sized concrete brick that can be laid mechanically. A mineral top layer allows the brick to retain its light-gray color. The surface includes stainless-steel anchor plates, which glisten in the sunlight, for use in setting up market stands. The market floor is laid out as an autonomous plane, which is linked to surrounding development by an anthracite-gray plinth. Because the composition of the market includes two aisles – which make it too long for the area in question and necessitate its extension into Hoogstraat – there is room for spacious pedestrian zones on both sides, as well as space for trees. Although on non-market days, Binnenrotte could function as a centrally located parking lot with an enormous capacity, the area is *not* part of the traffic-circulation network. A boundary consisting of 6-meter-long tubes, which can retract into recesses beneath the surface of the marketplace, prevents cars from entering the area.

THE CREATION OF INNER-CITY OPEN SPACE

Boompjes

Borough • CITY-CENTER
Designer • OMA, CEES CHRISTIAANSE; BUREAU B + B; dS+V
Artist • AUKE DE VRIES; FRED CARASSO; KUNST EN VAARWERK

Type of plan • QUAY
Qualitative level • EXCLUSIVE
Management level • REPRESENTATIVE
Surface area • 11.500 m²
Date planning began • 1985
Date of completion • 1989

Exploitation Boompjes • F 7.400.000,-
Layout costs • F 643,-/m²

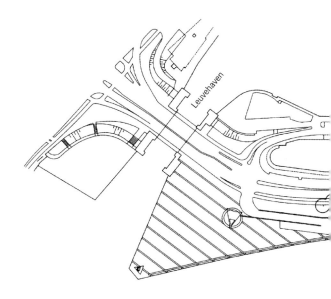

The river as stage for the Rotterdam Regatta.

Waterstad, the 'water city' included in the *1985 Inner-City Plan,* is located in the part of Rotterdam that lies along the Nieuwe Maas and is articulated by old harbor basins. The aim of the plan is to reinforce the water-related identity of this triangular area and to make it as attractive as possible for both residents and tourists. This aim is linked to another objective of the plan: the desire to improve the relationship between river and Centrumruit. Waterstad is conceptually divided into two kinds of areas: those perpendicular to the river, and those parallel to the river. The location of special recreational facilities lends a specific character to the axes. For example, Leuvehaven, which accommodates the Maritime Museum, the Maritime Open-Air Museum, and Imax (a panoramic motion-picture theater), has been developed as a promenade to the river.

The Boompjes, the old riverfront area from which elms have long since disappeared but from which the view of moored barges and ships gliding by is as sensational as ever, is the most important parallel route. Together, the dike above and the quay below form an arena of pageantry for the city on the river. Unlike the axes, the Boompjes includes flexible, rather than permanent, facilities, which offer a myriad of opportunities for use. The experience of an ever-flowing river is the most important 'use.' The river is there every morning for those skimming along the illuminated jogging track at the water's edge, but also for crowds sitting on the grandstand and enjoying a sailing exhibition, an orchestra on the quay, or fireworks over the water. The black-terrazzo arcade on the dike has electrical facilities for lighting and for sound installation, as well as attachments for a pavilion roof, which can cover the grandstand. When no special event is taking place, the arcade is an unpretentious, transparent element. Because the Boompjes is part of a system of dikes that have been raised to the minimum safe height, it is not (yet) possible to replant it with the several rows of trees it once had.

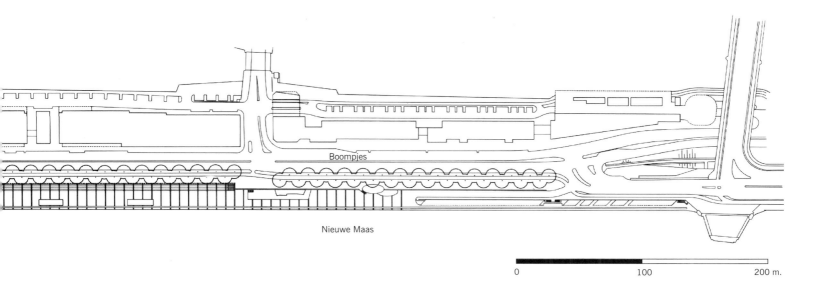

Boompjes

Nieuwe Maas

0   100   200 m.

THE CREATION OF INNER-CITY OPEN SPACE

The Kop van Zuid Project

ROSEPARK

CARGADOORPLEIN/BINNENHAVEN

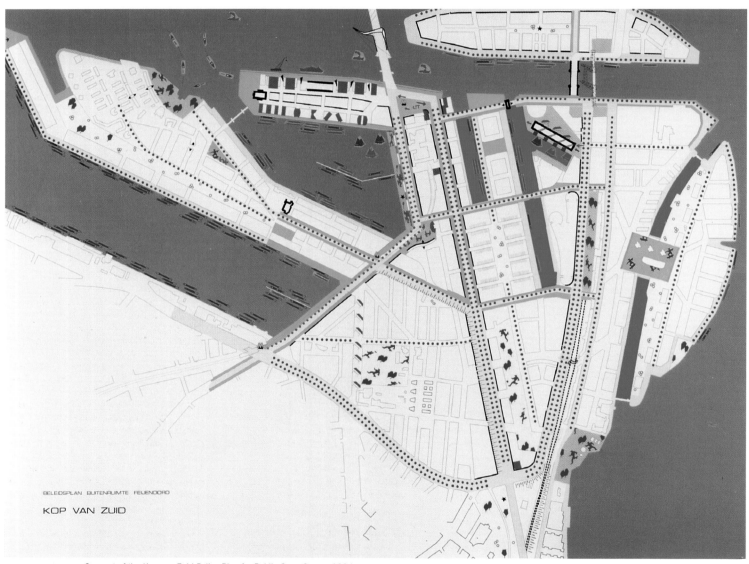

Concept of the Kop van Zuid Policy Plan for Public Open Space, 1994.

The Kop van Zuid is a large site covering 250 hectares, which includes harbor basins, former port industry, and warehouses, as well as an extensive railroad network that once served the port. In the 1970s and early '80s, several public-housing projects were developed in this area for the purpose of absorbing the overspill from urban-renewal projects in surrounding districts. Calculations showed that traditional housing would not generate enough money to cover the costs of acquiring and reorganizing this area. Directors of Rotterdam's Department of Urban Planning and the City Development Corporation recognized the area's potential. Situated across from the inner city, on a splendid inner bend of the Nieuwe Maas and virtually in the heart of Rotterdam, the site offered Rotterdam's neglected south side a fresh opportunity. A plan demonstrating the possibilities of the site was completed in 1987. The backbone of the plan is a new network of highways. A route accessing the area, which includes a viaduct that spans existing railroad lines, links national highways south of Rotterdam directly to the riverbank of the Wilhelmina Pier. Subsequently, a new bridge connects the area to the inner city and, in so doing, unites the two banks of the Maas right in the center of Rotterdam. On the left bank, a new metro station at the foot of the bridge will serve the existing metro line. The improved accessibility of the area is partially responsible for the development of high-quality housing and office buildings. Nineteenth-century harbor basins offer space for accompanying recreational

facilities. The organization of the project area also frees the surrounding residential districts of Feijenoord, Katendrecht, and Afrikaanderwijk from their isolated positions. In developing the master plan, designers created a number of important cross connections for this purpose. Central areas within these districts are linked to one another by way of the project area.

Commitment to Quality
With the reinforcement of Rotterdam's international position in mind, planners aimed for top quality throughout the entire area. In addition to incorporating the master plan within a development plan, three books of standards for quality were published. These so-called Q Books pertain to architecture, open space, and program. They offer a detailed amplification of the master plan for the various project areas and indicate characteristic features. Atmospheric and referential illustrations stimulate investors to develop high-quality architecture geared to other building projects and to public space. To ensure quality, a special committee responsible for building standards has been established; this body includes a number of prominent foreign advisers. Called the Q Team, it examines the municipality's urban plans, including architectonic plans and plans for public open space. The municipality is responsible for the quality of public space.
The Q Book for open space recommends various ambiences to be created within the project area. The northern section along the river is characterized as port city; promenades along nineteenth-century harbor basins form the most important open-space element. The focal point of the southern section is a centrally located park, which determines the ambience of a green residential area. A zone of development along the nineteenth-century district of Afrikaanderwijk breathes an atmosphere of narrow, compact streets and a number of squares. These milieus come to life in surfacing

materials, vegetation, and street furniture. Through its suggestions, the Q Book offers inspiration to private investors, as well as to various municipal departments and corporations. Unit prices set down in land-use plans are two to three times higher than those for standard areas. Serving as models for the quality desired, two project plans were realized in anticipation of the housing projects. On Pincoffsweg, next to the Peperklip, the square known as Cargadoorplein was redesigned, and quays along the Binnenhaven were restored. Results demonstrate the choice of a qualitative basis of durable, timeless materials for public space: paving stones with a basalt surface, the warm color of clinker bricks in the streets, and brick walls with ashlar coping blocks.

Coherence and Continuity
Concrete project plans are being developed for main roads and housing environment to accompany the first housing projects. Since the various parts of the Kop van Zuid project will be carried out according to a phased approach, and final plans only realized in 2010, the coordination of subplans is essential. Matters of continuity or contrast, coherence or particularization need to be determined for sectors, lines, and individual elements. The *Kop van Zuid Policy Plan for Public Open Space* was formulated to take care of such matters. It offers a framework for the continuity of profiles, differences in intensity of use, and the hierarchy of spatial units. Furthermore, the policy plan is an instrument that anchors the Kop van Zuid project within the organization of municipal departments. This relationship pertains not only to the design and realization, but also to the management of public space.
The relationship that links planned area, inner city, and surrounding districts is set down in the policy plan. Three north-south lines join the halves of the city. These lines are the city axis, which connects the area to Zuidplein via the

THE CREATION OF INNER-CITY OPEN SPACE

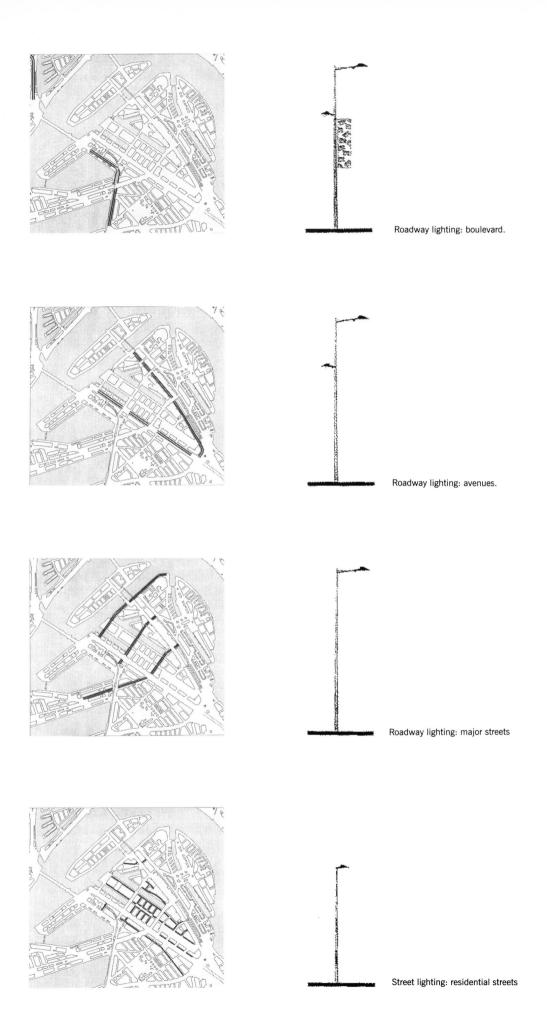

Roadway lighting: boulevard.

Roadway lighting: avenues.

Roadway lighting: major streets

Street lighting: residential streets

Erasmus Bridge; Emplacementsweg, the link to Varkenoordse Viaduct and the national highway, also via the Erasmus Bridge; and Rosestraat, which runs via Willems Bridge and Koninginnebrug (Queen Bridge) along the route taken by the railroad tunnel. At right angles to these lines are the cross connections, which join the area to Feijenoord and Katendrecht. The three main program-matic inner-city themes are also reflected on the Kop van Zuid. The entertainment aspect of Oude Haven's and Binnenrotte's sidewalk cafés and marketplace can be seen in the Entrepôt area. The inner city of high-rise construction, office buildings, and public functions continues across the water, via the Erasmus Bridge, on the Wilhelmina Pier. And finally, the triangle of museums, where art mingles with public space and verdant parks, has a subtle counterpart on the Kop van Zuid: a ferry connection across the Nieuwe Maas couples this area to the Wilhelmina Pier, which will accommodate public facilities such as an emigration museum. Estimates of annual maintenance costs for open space are based on information in the policy plan. These costs are comparable to present funds needed for the inner-city area on the right bank of the Maas: two to three times higher than for a standard

Impression of Wilhelminaplein by Peter Wilson, 1994.

residential area.

A selection of paving materials for the project area has been geared to the atmosphere of former harbor areas. Working principles have been developed for the use of selected paving materials; these principles include the most common standard applications, such as parking spaces and tree surrounds. A 30-centimeter-wide, anthracite-colored curbstone was chosen to go with the dark paving stone. To prevent loss of material from cutting and sawing, corner pieces will allow the use of standard-sized curbstones and paving tiles. Concrete setts measuring 97 by 97 millimeters - to correspond to the size of paving stones - will border tree surrounds and provide ventilation. Tree surrounds along highways will take the form of galvanized grids. The working principles, which correspond to project-plan budgets and to management requirements, form the basis for the dimensions and coherence of project plans for the Kop van Zuid.

The same operating procedure is being followed for street furniture. Attractive poles and fittings, which comply with functional and safety requirements for public lighting, will be used to illuminate areas for motorized and pedestrian traffic. The rest of the street furniture was also selected on the basis of good, functional design and does not exceed the limits of budgets for the realization and management of open space. To achieve a smooth transition between the Kop van Zuid and adjacent urban districts, certain elements will be carried over into Feijenoord, Katendrecht, and Noorder-eiland.

Particularization and Innovation

Apart from the basic layout, specific exceptions are indicated. These exceptions apply to the most important lines, areas, and intersections on the Kop van Zuid. The three north-south routes – city axis, Emplacementsweg, and Rosestraat – are to have special street lighting. A sand-colored sidewalk tile is being developed for the Wilhelmina Pier. The design of lighting, seating, and fencing will be coordinated to create a unique, coherent family of street furniture. And finally, plans include a number of special squares or hubs. One of these is Wilhelminaplein, the square at the foot of the new bridge to the Kop van Zuid. Peter Wilson designed the quay that borders the square. Special architectonic elements such as a colonnade, a tower of figures, electronic rocks, and a bridgekeeper's booth accentuate the significance of Wilhelminaplein as the entrance to Rotterdam South. With the use of special paving and street furniture, or a combination of the two, the exceptional spatial significance embodied by the project as a whole is expressed in its furnishings.

Following in the footsteps of examples in Barcelona and Paris, the Kop van Zuid project offers a new approach to public space. In addition to the importance of a centrally coordinated operation for the entire city, this project presents an exclusive approach to a confined urban area. Defining the Kop van Zuid as a special intracity project creates surplus energy. Each municipal department is asked to make a strong commitment. Standard solutions become the subject of debate: Why is it always done like this, and isn't there a better way? Extra effort is demanded of private investors as well. Utilities, refuse containers, and parking places are included in the new development. New paving materials, new street furniture, and new layout and maintenance techniques can be developed when the aim of all concerned is to achieve a higher level of quality. And ultimately, it is the city as a whole that profits from the broader scale of opportunities created by the existence of a model project for public space.

Rosepark

Submunicipality • FEIJENOORD
Designer • QUADRAT, PAUL ACHTERBERG

Type of plan • PARK
Qualitative level • EXCLUSIVE
Management level • INTENSIVE
Surface area • 13.000 m²
Date planning began • 1993
Date of completion • 1994

Apportionment fund • F 2.909.000,-
BSR-Fund • F 1.241.000,-
City Council Priority • F 500.000,-
Layout costs • F 357,-/m²

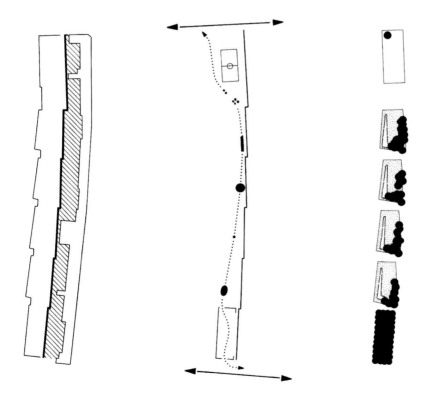

Wall separating public and private areas.

Route of play areas.

Rhythm of terraces.

Realization of the railroad tunnel made available an elongated site on the 'seam' between the Kop van Zuid and the district of Feijenoord. Because the train once ran past backyards belonging to the housing block on Oranjeboomstraat, the site - as viewed from the direction of Feijenoord - is isolated. Nevertheless, it now accommodates a park, since, for technical reasons pertaining to foundations, it could not be used for housing. Plan development for Rosepark is not included within the framework of the Kop van Zuid. The Q Book, however, does state that the park must be laid out to suit its location on Rosestraat, a busy main street.

Residents of Oranjeboomstraat were afraid that a park with little opportunity for social supervision would cause problems. For this reason, a great deal of attention was given to the distinction between the private atmosphere of people's homes and the public atmosphere of the park. This distinction took shape in the form of a revetment at the edge of the railroad-tunnel roof. The wall is clad with brick on the side facing the backyards and with basalt on the side facing the park. Because the park lies, for the most part, above the railroad tunnel, its design is highly architectonic. Basic qualities of the site - long, narrow, at right angles to the river - were called on to create a series of terraces, which ascend in a southerly direction. Because their surfaces have a slight incline, differences in elevation seem greater than they are; each terrace is connected to the following by three stairs. Furthermore, the perspective has been manipulated by segmenting the wall and by having the terraces follow the curve of Rosestraat. The highest terrace, which offers a view of bridges spanning the Maas, is covered with acacia trees, planted there to emphasize the opening of the tunnel. The lowest terrace, easily accessible from the district of Feijenoord, has a paved surface for ball games and roller-skating. The four intermediate terraces, with playgrounds for small children, are planted with Japanese raisin trees and holly.

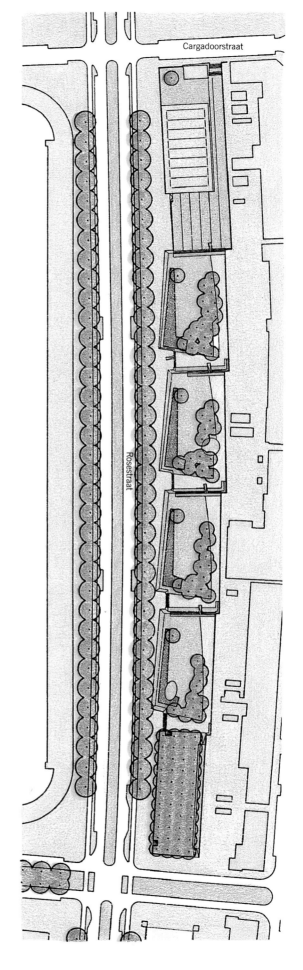

0   25   50 m.

THE CREATION OF INNER-CITY OPEN SPACE

Cargadoorplein/Binnenhaven

Submunicipality • FEIJENOORD
Designer • dS+V, PAUL ACHTERBERG

Type of plan • HOUSING ENVIRONMENT
Qualitative level • EXCLUSIVE
Management level • INTENSIVE
Surface area • 11.500 m²
Date planning began • 1991
Date of completion • 1993

Exploitation Kop van Zuid • F 2.000.000,-
Layout costs • F 174,-/m²

Binnenhaven is one of the late-nineteenth-century harbors to be transformed, within the framework of the Kop van Zuid project, from an industrial site into a central urban area for housing and employment. The perspective of the harbor basin (the entire length of which has been preserved), the characteristic *Poortgebouw* at its entrance, and the urban plan for the new city on the river serve as points of departure for a high-quality layout of public space. The edge of the basin consisted of all sorts of quays and banks, realized in various materials. It was an unkempt sight. To create a uniform image, new quays were designed. The western quay is treated as a long, continuous edge, which corresponds to the new urban structure on Landtong (the spit). The distinctive design of the eastern quay relates to the situation of a

large apartment building, the Peperklip, and to development on both sides of Entrepôthaven. The Q Book was consulted for details and choice of materials. After soil-sanitation operations had been completed and a new 'living layer' put in place on the western spit, ground level was higher than the existing quay. Because of the harbor basin's new function as a berth for inland vessels, and because the difference in tides measures 1.5 meters, raising the quay was not an option. The problem was solved by building a low revetment 6 meters from the quay. The 800-meter-long wall separates a lower-lying barge path and promenade from the parking lane above. Ramps corresponding to cross streets lend access to the lower level. The pale-red brick wall, with ashlar coping blocks, houses electrical facilities for the ships. This wall is topped by columns with lampposts and a curved, swan-shaped railing. The quay itself is made of basalt.
Because residents of the Peperklip had lived so long on an island amid a sea of large building sites and soil-sanitation projects, they were next in line - following completion of the railroad tunnel and new development - to be provided with an accelerated layout of open space around their complex. The area involved

includes a plateau on the water, as well as a new public square between the apartment complex and the bridge spanning Binnenhaven. This site formerly accommodated a nautical-equipment wharf, whose presence determined the shape of the Peperklip. Now that this operation no longer exists, there is a striking transition between public space and the semipublic area around the building: it is unclear where the street ends and the courtyard begins. To solve this problem, Cargadoorplein was designed to act as a counterbalance to the building. The planting grid accommodating a block of chestnut trees lies completely within the building lines of the curved walls; it does follow, however, the orientation of the harbor basin. Little walls along the border offer some protection to those walking in the open, windy area. Walls and curbs at the edge of the square are gray. The square is paved in yellow brick. Even though the square is an autonomous element, the color scheme given to its border and surface serves as a link to the architecture of the Peperklip. At the request of the residents, a roller-skating rink was added between tree-filled square and quay. This area has proved to be a favorite spot for young people to gather after school.

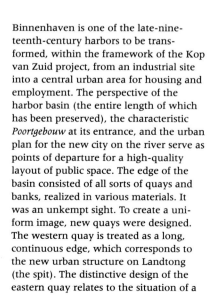

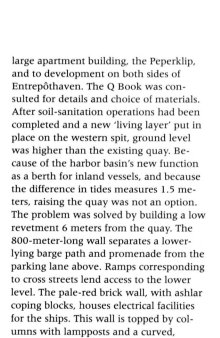

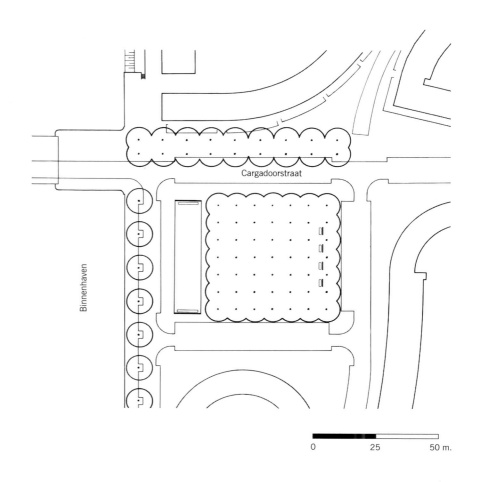

Cargadoorstraat

Binnenhaven

0   25   50 m.

THE CREATION OF INNER-CITY OPEN SPACE

Impression of canopies in Groene Hilledijk, by Van den Broek and Bakema, Barbara Starzynska, 1994.

Shopping Centers and Shopping Streets

Recent years have been characterized by a boom in renovations of, and investments in, shopping centers and shopping streets. Many shopping centers were built in the 1950s and '60s and are, just as their housing counterparts, in need of renovation. Moreover, shopping centers have captured the interest of corporate investors. Following the collapse of the market for office space, they found an attractive investment in shopping centers. An important feature in renovating shopping centers is open space. The relationship between the two is more important than it seems at first glance: open space offers a setting in which shops can present themselves. This relationship becomes clear only when the balance between public space and retail business is broken by over-

due maintenance or by conscious changes in one of the two components. An important characteristic of the relationship between shops and open space is the presence, in nearly every case, of multiple parties. Shops are owned either by one or more investors or by the people who operate them. In retail businesses that have been set up according to a systematic plan, such as those on Binnenban or Lijnbaan, those in charge of the shops are often tenants. On shopping streets such as West-Kruiskade, those running the businesses are generally the same people who own them. Open space is, in virtually every case, the responsibility of the municipality.

In systematically planned shopping centers, the initiative

that brings about change usually begins with the owner of the complex; if there are multiple owners, change is generally initiated by the municipality. A successful conversion process requires consultation. The municipality invites the parties involved to serve on a planning team, where, together with the initiator, they can exchange ideas that will lead to the benefit of all. In most cases, owners and investors are interested in a higher return. Operators want to see an improvement in competitive position and earnings. The municipality has a much broader range of objectives, from the support of economic initiatives – with a view to maintaining facilities – to the simple beautification of open space or the improvement of mutual relationships between various parts of a shopping area. In practice, since some interests carry more weight than others, the conversion process seldom runs smoothly. The owner with conversion plans has to convince his tenants of their benefit. After changes have been made, these tenants often face an increase in rent. And who guarantees them a higher return as well? A shop rarely undergoes changes that do not also affect the surrounding open space; is the municipality prepared to invest at this moment? And is the owner or tenant prepared to accept the new situation and to take responsibility for maintenance?

Three investment scenarios can be distinguished. The first is one in which the municipality is involved with more than one major owner-landlord. In this case, intensive collaboration is the option most often selected. The second scenario pertains to the renovation of systemically planned shopping centers that are owned and rented out by one person. The owner takes the initiative and the municipality either does or does not participate. The third investment scenario is found in the classic shopping street with many owner-occupants. As a rule, the municipality initiates renovation and the decision to participate lies with the owners.

The most intensive form of collaboration, and one in which risks are shared, is public-private partnership. The various participants have substantial interests, which correspond fairly well. This form of investment is often seen in complex situations in which financial risks are high; investments of this sort are usually in the multimillions. In such cases, the municipal government often works with one or more important private parties. A current example of this form of investment is the Beursplein (Stock Exchange Square) project. The municipality and the developer have collaborated closely on this project from the outset. Both parties wanted to boost the quality of the area. Without collaboration, the project would not have got off the ground. New open space that resulted from this partnership makes up part of the complex development. The Kruiskade project proves that public-private partnership does not *always* involve multimillion-guilder operations. The buildings had already been realized when the investor discovered that the condition of adjacent open space did not live up to high ambitions held for the buildings. Consequently, the investor

suggested to the municipality that they work together to improve this open space.

Most shopping centers have a single owner-landlord or, in the case of more than one, a Proprietors' Association (PA). Generally speaking, this party initiates investments. To make renovation cost-effective, it is almost always combined with the addition of more shops. Examples of similar investments are recently renovated shopping centers in Hoogvliet and IJsselmonde: Binnenban and Keizerswaard, respectively. Following renovation, it is often possible for the owner or PA to renew leases with retail merchants and to increase the rent, creating a situation in which the shopping center as a whole becomes an attractive marketable object. If the interests of those participating are more divergent, the parties involved often opt to collaborate on plan development, but to deal with investments separately.

In each case, results may vary. The owners of both Binnenban and Keizerswaard were aiming for high quality: public space with marble tiles. Nevertheless, the municipal investment norm for both centers was at the 'standard-plus' level. This norm was not high enough to satisfy the owners' goals. Subsequently, the municipal standard-plus level was raised a bit for the Binnenban project; the shopping center was provided with the same kind of tiles used on Coolsingel. The mall section of Keizerswaard, which is part of the open-space area, was given 'for nothing' to the owner, who then installed the marble tiles himself.

Shopping streets are most often the object of divided ownership. The shopkeepers' association will not rush to initiate improvements, because such a step always costs its members money. Such investments are usually substantial, and higher returns for individual shopkeepers are uncertain. Here lies an important role for the municipality, which can step in, as initiator and coordinator, to upgrade the appearance of the shopping street. Reasons may vary. The most frequent incentive preceding the integral improvement of shopping streets is periodic maintenance or the raising of streets and tramlines. Another reason might be the renovation of private housing. The degree to which shopkeepers lend a hand differs quite a bit. At times their role is extremely limited, such as on Nieuwe Binnenweg, where the shopkeepers' association paid for nothing but new flags. In other cases, their contribution is greater, such as on Beijerlandselaan, where shopkeepers were persuaded to install new awnings.

Kruiskade

Borough • CITY-CENTER
Designer • dS+V

Type of plan • SHOPPING STREET
Qualitative level • SELECT
Management level • REPRESENTATIVE
Surface area • 3.600 m²
Date planning began • 1991
Date of completion • 1994

General Fund • F 325.000,-
Nonmunicipal financing • F 85.000,-
Layout costs • F 114,-/m²

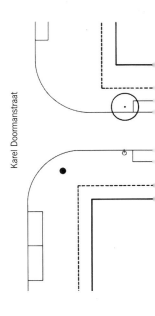

Karel Doormanstraat

The introduction of one-way streets and a guided parking system has resulted in better-regulated traffic within the Centrumruit and, as a result, more and more space for pedestrians. Kruiskade, long an animated area enlivened by shops, cafés, restaurants, and theaters, is now an example of an urban street in which the relationship between the domain of cars and that of pedestrians has altered since the one-way policy was adopted.
Broad sidewalks dominate the streetscape, the roadway is narrower than it was, and parking places have been reorganized. Paving materials here are the same as those used throughout the city center; they form a neutral backdrop for a number of special additions. Above-average quality has been achieved through a well-balanced application of exceptional elements. Ten sycamore maples have been planted on the north side. Along with ten eye-catching lampposts on the south side, these trees determine Kruiskade's new look, day and night. Three special areas ornament the pavement: a wooden platform, which can serve as an outdoor café; a strip of marble tiles, which indicates the entrance to several restaurants; and a 'garden' of green tiles that can accommodate plant containers and potted palms. New street furniture also includes a few handsome benches and a couple of logo posts. Particularizations in the streetscape are the result of public-private partnership. The owner and manager of real estate lining the street contributed substantially to boosting the quality of Kruiskade's public open space.

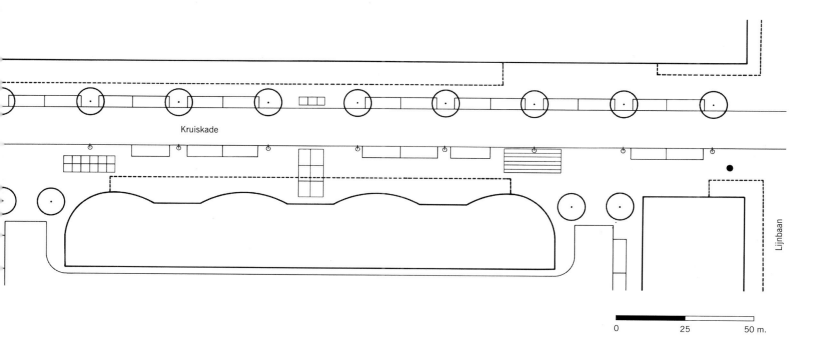

Kruiskade

Lijnbaan

0 25 50 m.

Binnenban Shopping Center

Submunicipality • HOOGVLIET
Designer • dS+V, JOHAN GOOSSENS
Artist • CHRIS ELFFERS

Type of plan • SHOPPING CENTER
Qualitative level • SELECT
Management level • INTENSIVE
Surface area • 10.400 m²
Date planning began • 1992
Date of completion • 1993 - 1994

Exploitation Hoogvliet-Center • F 1.400.000,-
City-council priority • F 1.000.000,-
Layout costs streets • F 65,-/m²
Layout costs shopping center • F 226,-/m²

Just as many shopping centers built in the 1960s, Binnenban in Hoogvliet has quite a spacious layout. Too spacious, because the complex ultimately realized was not the same as the larger one originally planned.

Deterioration of the building complex led to the owner's decision to renovate the shopping center and the housing above it. When the submunicipality learned of the proposal for renovation, it enthusiastically supported the project, on condition that plans would also include open space. Finding funds to finance the entire project presented a problem, especially when it came to reorganizing public space, but a substantial contribution from the municipality finally set the stage to proceed. The architecture firm formulated a plan in which approximately 6,000 square meters of public space was converted into rentable retail premises. New shops were placed against blank facades, a new building was erected in the northeast corner, and a small, pavilion-like building now stands in the middle of the shopping-center courtyard – a diagonal element with a mind of its own. New awnings reinforce architectonic unity. The reduction of public space – particularly the narrowing of connective routes throughout the shopping area – called for a good pedestrian network. Paving patterns and materials divide the area into zones, each with its own function. Thus shopkeepers may display goods outside their shops only on a strip of concrete bricks that runs along the facades. Next to this strip is a broad, obstacle-free zone intended for shoppers. This zone is composed of pink concrete slabs known as Bavarian granite. A relaxation area with benches and trees surrounds the pavilion. This zone is paved in a striped pattern. To the west, outside the complex, the sidewalk – much broader now and bordered by a zone for street furniture, trees, market stalls, and small sidewalk cafés – forms a good spatial transition: from the intimate shopping courtyard to shops, restaurants, and cafés outside the complex, and then on to the newly organized parking lot.

Since the renovation, the shopping center has attracted a much larger public; even people from neighboring municipalities find their way to this extremely modern shopping area in Hoogvliet. Free parking for customers stimulates this interest.

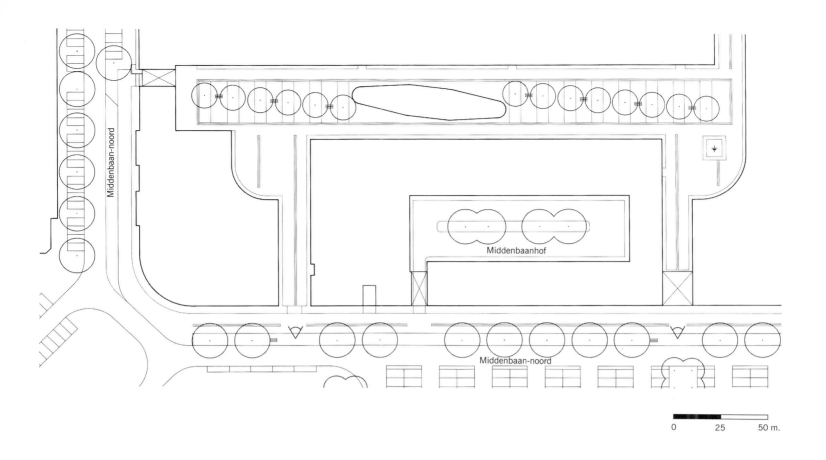

Middenbaan-noord

Middenbaanhof

Middenbaan-noord

0   25   50 m.

113

West-Kruiskade

Borough • CITY-CENTER
Designer • dS+V, RIA AARNINK

Type of plan • SHOPPING STREET
Qualitative level • SELECT
Management level • INTENSIVE
Surface area • 18.000 m²
Date planning began • 1992
Date of completion • 1994

SOR-Fund • F 1.000.000,-
City-council Priority 92/95 • F 800.000,-
Layout costs • F 100,-/m²

West-Kruiskade is one of the most important thoroughfares linking the city center and districts in the west; the street is part of a long, extremely busy ribbon of shops and hospitality-industry concerns. The combination of these two functions is spatially problematic. Roadway, parking lanes, and raised tramline take up so much room that there is no place for cycle lanes and minimum space for narrow sidewalks. In the past, pedestrians using the sidewalk were hindered by a lot of street furniture, billboards, and outdoor retail displays. When it became necessary to replace poles supporting tram wires and, at the same time, to raise the sidewalks, the municipality, seeing an opportunity to improve the general layout of the street, took the initiative in setting up meetings that included its own people, the tram company, the power company, and the shopkeepers' association.

It proved impossible to change the layout of the street; the solution had to be found in an efficient use of the sidewalk. The most important improvement is the introduction of the *multimast,* a pole supplying power for street lighting as well as for the tramline. By providing a place for traffic signs, litter bins, and advertisements posted by shops, such poles free the sidewalk to a large degree. Realization of this principle, however, was not simple. First, a fixed linear measurement had to be calculated - along one line - for the placement of poles and trees. In the case of West-Kruiskade, calculating a suitable module was extremely difficult because of the many irregularly spaced side streets and the network of cables and pipes beneath the sidewalk. Poles and trees had to be placed in the parking lane. And second, both the purchase and maintenance of the poles required the creation of good agreements involving all parties concerned. The tram company bought the poles and assumes responsibility for their maintenance, the power company helps to finance that maintenance, and the shopkeepers pay for banners bearing the street logo, which are attached to the poles. Keeping in mind the narrow width of the sidewalks, the municipality opted for gray concrete paving bricks. To achieve overall unity in the design, anti-parking bollards at the curb sport black and blue stripes, as do the poles.

Street furniture prior to 1993.

Straat furniture after1993.

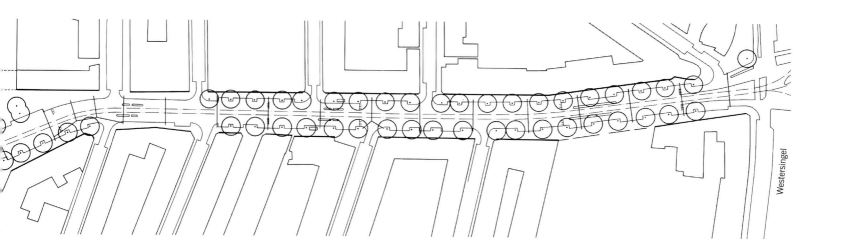

Westersingel

SHOPPING CENTERS AND SHOPPING STREETS

'The principal idea is that an accessible ground floor will have a motivational effect on the use of the second floor'

An interview with Lionel Coombs, project-director of the Utrecht City-Center Project Development Company

'THE FIRST OBJECTIVE of the Utrecht City-Center Project is the improvement of public space in the area that includes Jaarbeursplein, Utrecht's Central Station, and Hoog-Catharijne shopping mall. Other goals pertain to the development of the business center, the mall, and the public-transportation hub. But realization, use, and management of public space occupy center stage. All the actors in this area – the Municipality of Utrecht, the Dutch Railroad Company [NS], real-estate owners and users - have rallied to support these goals. This solidarity has its origins in the conviction that a clear relationship exists between the practical value of this area for the population and the commercial yields to be gained by those in business.

This relationship also lies at the foundation of the concept for Hoog-Catharijne: an attractive, covered, second-story shopping route between station and inner city. The ground floor was designed to accommodate through traffic, and two shopping arcades on the second floor serve to link station and city center. Hoog-Catharijne has proved itself a success, but the negative side is also evident. I see the UCP first and foremost as a challenge to improve the concept by adding a dimension to the ground-floor. The principal idea is that an accessible ground floor will have a motivational effect on the use of the second floor. Planned adaptations should also allow more people to be accommodated than before, and in a pleasant manner.

Other than the municipality, the initial impetus for development of the area came from three enterprises: the Trade-Fair Center; APB, owner of Hoog-Catharijne; and the NS. Their initiative led to the Master Plan of 1993. On the basis of this plan, the city council decided to establish a public-private partnership, or PPP, which has the resources to fully develop and realize the master plan. All parties in the PPP share equally the risks connected to land development. Such an agreement is necessary, because the improvement of public space in this area, given its existing structure, demands gigantic investments in the creation of favorable conditions. For example: making the area accessible to slow-moving traffic means finding a place for cars. For this group of users, we're creating space underground. Streets will be vaulted, and we'll build parking garages. Such operations are very expensive.

In issuing the Master Plan, the project's boosters have completed their task. Layout of public open space is not their nuclear role. After all, the Trade-Fair Center is primarily a marketing affair, the NS a means of transportation, and the APB an investor. They've retreated to their own spheres, from which they make their investments, as agreed in the plan. As everyone can see, the NS is already totally immersed in activity. The current PPP includes other, commercial development companies, which will be able to use parts of the newly available space. Thus the creation of public space leads to extremely well-situated, high-quality functions. This interaction is the essence of the project.

Programmatic components of the plan, which must support quality, are not hierarchically related to one another. To begin with, this city needs a large, centrally located square. What if FC Utrecht wins the Cup this year? The mayor would have a hard time finding a spot where he could welcome the team and address the fans. The development of a square or plaza is, therefore, one of our objectives. Second, Central Station is tucked away out of sight, invisible to cyclists and pedestrians and inaccessible to motorized traffic. This is not good; a station should be a beacon, an orientation point within the city. A third matter is the safety of our citizens. This is not the best place to be after dark. Whether or not it's safe here, however, isn't the real issue: it makes people feel unsafe. Improper use is made of the area in a number of ways, and there's a prevailing sense that when you're here, your belongings are not your own. We're going to eliminate that feeling as well as possible. Fourth, retail business needs room to expand. We're going to provide that room. And fifth, the public transportation network is due to be revised. This phenomenon exhibits an autonomous growth that will become even greater in the coming years as a result of major urban-expansion activities in the region.

In realizing the plan, we're aiming for unity in diversity. Public space will have to be designed in an extremely differentiated way, without losing sight of coherence. For inspiration, we've gone to other countries to study comparable projects. Experiences there have reinforced my theory that we should look for solutions made to size. The task we face demands specific expertise and skill. The perception of space is, furthermore, a culturally determined factor. A Dutch person experiences and uses a square in an entirely different way than does a Spaniard or an Italian. In order to guarantee this cultural dimension, I tend to look for Dutch designers. Foreign projects and architects provide me with a source of inspiration; you learn from one another - it's reciprocal. This means that Dutch designers must continue to have the opportunity to show how spatial design can be used to tie into the collective frame of reference in this country. I'm arguing, therefore, not for a provincial, close-minded ideology, but for openness, the objective being to inspire – not to copy – one another.

We're now in the process of assembling the various parts of the project. Still to come are consultations with administrators, concerned parties, and city residents, followed by the drafting of a Development Plan, which, in this context, can be compared to the UCP Investment Plan for the coming 10 to 15 years. The plan, scheduled to be completed in early 1996, forms the basis of the municipal zoning plan, which will follow customary procedures.'

Master plan for the Utrecht City-Center Project, 1993.

'We do things a little bit slower now, but we're doing an outstanding job'

An interview with Hans Dona, former alderman for the Department of Physical Planning, Municipality of 's-Hertogenbosch, and currently director of the Brabant Pers (Brabant Press)

'THE INNER CITY OF 's-HERTOGENBOSCH suffered greatly during the final years of the war, but its structure remained intact. Economically, the postwar years weren't easy, and that's why little money was invested in the beginning. In the 1960s, a new hospital, a police station, and a fire station were built in the Tolbrugkwartier adjacent to the old city center; this was seen as an overture to renewed urban élan. The structure plan of 1964 established a much farther-reaching ambition for renovation of the inner city. This plan provided for the creation of traffic breakthroughs, new parking facilities, plenty of room and top priority for tradespeople, no additional housing, and the filling-in of the Dieze, which was an unsafe sewer at the time.

Protests from residents put a stop to the process and even brought about political repercussions. Mobilized sentiments in support of the historical quality of the old city center led to waning intentions; the result is that 's-Hertogenbosch still has its Uylenburgh and its Binnendieze, among other things. Unlike the situation in Breda and Eindhoven, large-scale restoration projects failed to appear. Small-scale improvements and adaptations continued to be made, but never a genuinely fundamental restructuring. Since the 1970s, the prevailing view has been that the inner city is really worth the effort. Government reports since then advise the purchase of monuments and the restoration of, for example, the city walls. The question has come up as to whether the use of Eindhoven as a frame of reference shouldn't be replaced by something else. The urban-planning quality of the inner city is determined by the structure of the old city, with its double triangle of city walls and marketplace, and, between the points of the triangles, the connective streets; the closed, slightly curved building lines; and the heights of the facades.

In a city like 's-Hertogenbosch, we have only a small number of authentic monuments. Sint-Jan, for instance, the citadel, the Moriaan. The strength of the inner city lies – to a much greater extent – in its urban-planning structure, in the ensemble quality. In the course of the '70s, the desire to respect this coherent situation was elevated to a general policy, which was implemented in the '80s by buying and restoring various buildings. In many cases, municipal initiatives formed the impetus for private improvements. This chain of events resulted in a decidedly restored shopping function and led to a gradual improvement of the housing function.

There are few office buildings in the center of 's-Hertogenbosch. It has never been an industrial city, but rather a mercantile center with an administrative profile. Its large-scale complexes are service institutions and cloisters. An excellent illustration of the solicitous treatment given to the inner city since the '60s is the decision to have the provincial government building, designed by Maaskant, erected in 's-Hertogenbosch South, next to the highway. Even then, the thought was that high-rise buildings were no longer acceptable. Recently, the municipality was faced with a comparable problem: our judicial branch wanted to realize a sizable extension on the city wall, overlooking the Bossche Broek. After a great deal of shilly-shallying, we managed – with the help of the Government Building Agency – to persuade them to move into available space next to the station, in new buildings that are part of the La Gare Plan, designed by Charles Vandenhoven. This may appear to be on the periphery of the inner city, but, at the same time, you have to realize that the inner city is expanding. In addition, maintaining a strict hierarchy of shopping centers has been of great importance to the revitalization of the inner city. Up to now, the municipality has resisted the introduction of big supermarkets and peripheral retail business. Shopping centers in residential districts satisfy the need for daily supplies; the entire segment above that level is found in the city center. No Hema or V&D department stores in the districts, only in the heart of the city. The improvement in quality has now been developed to such a degree that 's-Hertogenbosch also attracts those who do "recreational shopping." In the meantime, we know that the visitor to the inner city stays for a relatively long time: people like the warm atmosphere here. Once more, not because of big commercial drawing cards, such as the Bijenkorf department store, but, on the contrary, because of the broad selection of high-quality shops. A notch higher than shops in Eindhoven, Nijmegen, and Tilburg.

The Municipality of 's-Hertogenbosch is behaving more and more like an active party on the rise. We've taken the plan for open space in the inner city squarely on our own financial shoulders. For 20 years after the war had ended, there was so little faith in the quality of the city that third parties seldom wanted to invest their money. Perhaps this explains why we've learned to take responsibility for our own problems. In the case of Loeffplein – there, too, we had the urban-planning criteria on paper before sitting down at the table with partners to discuss and collaborate on further developments.

In recent years the municipality has continued to look for expansion space in which to locate city-center facilities, and, in so doing, it began to consider the aforementioned Tolbrugkwartier. Large-scale functions from the '60s were never suitable for this spot, which lies 100 meters from the marketplace. It's simply a bad area. We asked two Spanish architects, Oscar Tusquets and Beth Gali, to design a plan for Tolbrugkwartier. We asked the same thing of a private partner who has a feeling for the coherence between this new development and the rest of the city center. Together, they'll realize the fourth shopping axis: Marktstraat-Loeffplein. To prevent this development from leading to the neglect of other areas, the shopkeepers' association decided to establish an Inner-City Management Council, which assumed responsibility for boosting – in a differentiated manner – the quality of the entire city center. At that moment, it became clear that investments in public space were the means by which to carry out well-considered projects within the historical urban core. An inventorial study done by B+B Consultancy has given us insight into the physical position and functioning of open-space areas. The study formed a basis for calling in Beth Gali. She designed the recently laid out Kerkplein.

We have not taken refuge in verdure. The inner city is characterized by extreme urban density and, as such, is unsuitable as a place for greenery. This can be found in nearby Zuiderpark, for which a new reorganizational plan has also been developed. Our goal in ameliorating the inner city is to improve the connection to the Parade and surrounding residential districts, and to enhance the way the core functions internally. Apart from that, such plans release a flood of intense emotions. It seems that most modifications can be justified only after they're realized. On the basis of a plan, it's hard to convince people. Ever since the '60s, conservatism has been flowing through the blood of our population. Being ambitious quickly took on a negative connotation here. The same negativity forms the backdrop for the fact that no real architectonic wonders are to be found here. On the one hand, residents are

proud and somewhat chauvinistic, but such emotions are not expressed in the kind of élan evident in Rotterdam. I think Kerkplein is an important step in the right direction. We do things a little bit slower now in 's-Hertogenbosch, but for the first time, we're doing an outstanding job.'

Impression of the reorganization of Kerkplein in 's-Hertogenbosch, by Beth Gali, 1994.

Urban Renewal

Old Squares

At the beginning of the nineteenth century, Rotterdam consisted of two areas, each with a different character. The port area, which was outside the Schiedamsedijk (dike) and Hoogstraat (retaining wall), and which accommodated a thorough blend of housing and harbor activities, was also known as Waterstad (Water City). Landstad (Land City) lay within the dikes, between moats known as Coolse Vest and Goudse Vest, and formed an extremely concentrated housing and employment area, which was originally crisscrossed by numerous ditches and watercourses. Various enterprises for which there was no room in Landstad – truck farms and lanen – were located outside the moats. Lanen were garden complexes in which prosperous residents of Rotterdam

spent their leisure time. The canals that City Architect Rose conceived as part of the water project of 1842 were designed as spacious elements to surround these gardens. The canals formed a new boundary between Landstad and Waterstad and villas located in the polders. Along the canals, greenery, footpaths, and bridle paths designed by the Zocher family gave the boundary the function of a recreational route. One side provided a view of green expansion area within the polder, and the other looked out over a panoramic landscape. Owing to the lovely surroundings and good accessibility, the Zochers recommended the land along the canals as an ideal location for building villas. Selling expensive parcels for this purpose would help to pay for realization of

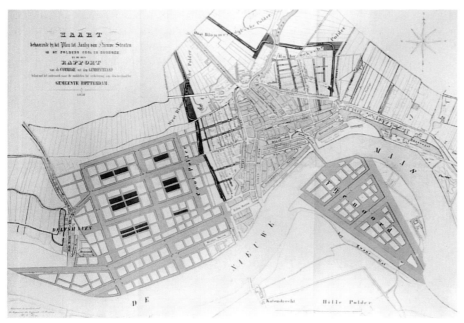

Plan of 1858, designed by Rose.

the canals. In conceiving this plan, however, Rose and the Zochers failed to anticipate Rotterdam's rapid development as a center of trade. This development followed the completion of the Nieuwe Waterweg (New Waterway: 1862-1872) and was soon accompanied by an enormous growth in population. In subsequent decades, the polder city experienced a sharp rise in housing density, and the city expanded in leaps and bounds, even beyond the canals.

The Nieuwe Waterweg reinforced the development of the city in an east-west direction as well. Rose, whose first priority was the spatial coherence of city and port, responded to the significance that the navigational route held for this development. He drew a model city for the island of Feijenoord; this model, which was a mirror image of the historical urban triangle on the opposite side of the Maas, created a new, north-south city axis. A monumental city bridge linked the two sides. Rose's plan was the first to span the Maas. Thus was created the future urban area of Rotterdam South.

During the period that Rose's successor, De Jongh, was responsible for urban development, the population of Rotterdam tripled, traffic increased significantly, and a separation occurred between the port and housing areas. To De Jongh, who was the director of Public Works from 1879 to 1910, the growth of port and city was chiefly a question of organization and logistics. During his term of office, the harbors of Rijnhaven and Maashaven were realized on the left bank of the Maas, and the railroad line from Amsterdam to Dordrecht was completed. The 'elevated railroad' ran straight across the existing city and followed, for a large part, the route of the Binnenrotte. De Jongh put his ideas on public space into practice in his design for broad streets and canals, which included space for future developments, such as railroad lines. Although De Jongh's canals had no

paths for outings by carriage, they formed an element of boulevards meant for use as important traffic routes. The streets next to Heemraadssingel and Essenburgsingel were designed as fast connections between working-class districts in the northwest and harbors in the south. In the *Expansion Plan for Coolpolder*, De Jongh limited himself to that which was feasible from a marketing standpoint, namely, the establishment of major lines. Along with Heemraadssingel, these were 's-Gravendijkwal, a tree-lined boulevard running north-south; Mathenesserlaan, a tree-lined boulevard running east-west; and a newly projected harbor, which was to become Coolhaven. Further development was left to private parties. Prominent merchants, industrialists, and dignitaries lived along main transportation routes and broad main streets such as Claes de Vrieselaan, which were also provided with trees and median strips. Somewhat less distinguished housing lined the narrower cross streets. Along the elegant course of Mathenesserlaan, which offered space among the plane trees to railroad traffic, the spirit of Art Nouveau was introduced. This new, late-nineteenth-century architecture, which had broken with neoclassic tradition completely, graced the facades of the boulevard and lent expression to the flourishing seaport and center of trade. Next to the intersection of Mathenesserlaan and Heemraadssingel, De Jongh designed the distinguished public garden of Heemraadsplein. This garden also marked the beginning of the part of Heemraadssingel that formed the second section of the planned beltway and that was even broader than the first stretch.

Although De Jongh was able to exercise a firm grip on developments in the port area and to have built, under his directorship, lovely neighborhoods for wealthy citizens and the bourgeoisie, he failed to corner the explosively growing market for working-class housing. There were quick profits to be made in this market, owing to the great shortage and high rents, certainly as long as the government issued no regulations. Vast working-class districts, financed by speculators, began arising both west and east of the City Triangle in the 1890s. This expansion was determined by the direction taken by units of subdivision known as *slagen* and by the distance between polder ditches. A road was laid out between the ditches; subsequently, lots at right angles to the road were sold and developed. Main access roads were formed by old country lanes. Existing ribbon development was included in the new development, and through routes evolved into retail ribbon development. Public space was determined exclusively by the narrow streets, within which all public activity took place. All things considered, the quality of these new working-class housing projects was not much better than it had been in Landstad. Dwellings were small, cramped, and dark. The drainage and sewer systems, which had been planned in advance, were the only improvements.

Developments on the left bank of the Maas were compara-

Heemraadssingel, 1922.

Mathenesserlaan, 1930.

ble to those on the right bank. Afrikaanderwijk, a district realized in Hillepolder to accommodate working-class housing for people employed in the new harbors, Rijnhaven and Maashaven, was developed with the underlying landscape in mind. Existing streets, such as Brede Hilledijk and Korteweg, became main access roads. Between them rose a housing area consisting of long, straight streets; high, narrow housing blocks; and little public verdure. Only Putselaan, a broad street to the south that forms a principal urban 'line,' was provided with trees and a median strip that accommodates railroad tracks.

As a result of rapid urban expansion, plans for a row of villas with gardens along Rose's canals were never realized as such, nor did the canals become, in all cases, obvious public areas for residents of the new districts. A number of developments took place. The southern part of Westersingel was linked to Westerdijk. This dike, which Rose had provided with greenery, formed a connection to the Park and to the first and second Nieuwe Werk, also designed by Rose. This shipping quarter – a continuation of the Boompjes – was meant to be an aesthetic and representative expansion of Rotterdam's port front. Between the park-like expansion and the distinguished shipping quarter, several freestanding villas were indeed built along the southern part of Westersingel. The northern section was lined with urban facades, in the form of tall, uninterrupted town houses. In Rotterdam West, the residential districts behind such 'golden borders' were concealed, almost entirely, from the canal areas. Only the retail ribbon development crossed the canals and linked expansion areas to the city center. In the northeastern section, still other developments were taking place along the canals. Here, farther away from the harbors, large open areas of the urban fabric remained available. These were used as sites for urban functions that needed a great deal of space. Town houses were also built along Boezemsingel, Crooswijksesingel, and Noordsingel, but at these places an abundance of cross streets provided a more closely interwoven relationship with densely built-up residential areas to the rear. In Noordsingel's bend, next to the Rotte, the Zochers designed a broad site, which was to be a special riverside location for villas. Their intentions were never realized, however. The green area became a busy hub, linking the districts of Oude Noorden, Crooswijk, and Rubroek; a bridge spanning the Rotte was built on this spot, at which many streets converged. Thus was Noordplein created. Increasing traffic, along with changing tastes, led to an adaptation in the layout of the canals themselves. Verdure became more 'urban,' and at places where main routes into the city intersected with canals, parts of the canals were filled in. An example is the hub next to the Rotte: in 1892, Noordsingel's bend was transformed into a public garden transected by a street. Owing to its location among the districts, the garden was later converted into a market square with a paved surface and a street surrounding it.

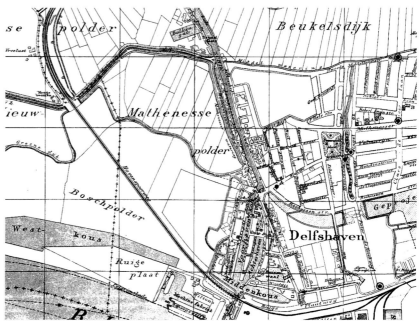

Detail of the map of Rotterdam, 1903.

The Planned Districts

When the Housing Act of 1901 was passed, public housing became the responsibility of the government. From that time forward, government would regulate the quality of housing and housing environments in working-class residential districts. As a result of this act, municipalities were required to design expansion plans, which would allow the activities of builders and developers to be steered in the right direction. In 1903 De Jongh designed the *First General Expansion Plan*, which specified the future development of Rotterdam. His plan for Spangensepolder and Mathenesserpolder still followed, to a large degree, the orientation of the historical subdivision into *slagen*.

The adoption of the Housing Act stimulated the administration's willingness to improve housing conditions. A Municipal Housing Department was established; beginning in 1910, under the leadership of Director Plate, many experiments were carried out using new types of housing and subdivision, both of which provided better housing conditions. One example is an improved incidence of natural light in public housing. Good housing conditions also included healthful open space. More attention was given to the area allotted to courtyards, as well as to public space between housing blocks. In realizing a plan for streets and buildings with enough open space to serve an entire district, the difficulty of acquiring land in a strained housing market posed a problem. Civil-engineering preparations and the drainage of new expansion areas such as Spangen took so much time that speculation became a threat. For this reason, the municipality began buying land covertly, at an early stage, for new western expansion areas meant to accommodate the harbors of Lekhaven and IJsselhaven. Of the working-class districts planned, Bospolder was developed first, followed by Spangen and, finally, Tussendijken, because land here was

in the hands of one speculator.

Open space played a role in the development of a district's individual identity. Bospolder's concentric composition and diagonal main streets made the district a recognizable entity. The center of the district consisted of an area filled with a freestanding school building and a square bordered by trees: Bospolderplein. Burgdorffer's plan for Spangen (1913) was an elaboration of De Jongh's general design. In laying out streets and building blocks within this general design, the old subdivision into *slagen* was no longer relevant. To create a sense of social solidarity, Spangen became home to soccer club Sparta. It was the club's training fields, located on both sides of the splendid Kasteel Stadium and at the end of a formal termination of the extended central axis, that introduced a breath of fresh air between the housing blocks. And finally, the triangle of Tussendijken was designed with blocks parallel to the highways. Between them lay parcels of land at right angles to the dike. The lack of an official district center, with a square or some special element for residents, can be blamed, perhaps, on the situation surrounding ownership of the land.

On the left bank of the Maas, the search for new types of public housing took various forms. In the garden village of Vreewijk, open space served the vital function of lending a village-like identity to this expansion area so far away from the city. Vreewijk developed into a large district, with even streets and watercourses that link it to surrounding expansion areas. Canals on the left bank of the Maas, which are part of De Jongh's plan, are important connective elements within this integration. Hillevliet, realized under De Jongh's supervision, was extended to the south in the form of the Lange Geer, and a side branch of this extension, the Lede, is part of the Vreewijk plan. Districts that developed between Afrikaanderwijk and Vreewijk consisted of the same kind of

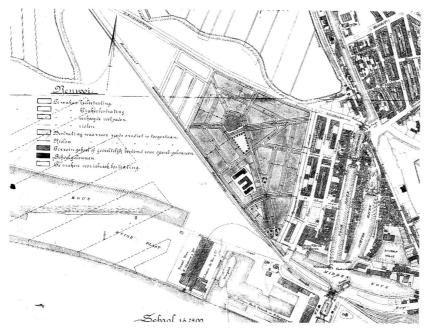
Plan of Bospolder by G.J. de Jongh, 1903.

low-rise buildings – with a foundation of steel piling – found
in Vreewijk. Because the municipality was the motor behind
such development, Bloemhof is also referred to as the municipal garden village. Here, too, housing had both front and
rear gardens. Unlike Vreewijk, public space took on a more
formal and urban character. Housing density was higher,
and streets, squares, and public gardens joined the urban
plan to form a unit. Examples are Balsiemplein, Bloemhofplein, and Heer Jansweg. These were not given a distinct
social function, such as their counterparts in Vreewijk,
Spangen, and Bospolder, where the creation of a sense of
community was considered essential. The image projected
by these newer open-space areas was more one of the pride
of working-class Rotterdammers in their housing environment, here in this seaport and center of trade.

Renovation of the Squares

The old squares are found in various urban locations. Some
are found at busy traffic intersections, others form the heart
of a district, and still others have the character of a
neighborhood square. What these squares have in common
is that their layouts and furnishings have changed over the
years, and that new developments have led, time and again,
to adaptations of their designs. Many times, the necessity for
new plans was a result of urban renewal. Buildings with
new functions gave rise to new forms of use for surrounding
open space. Changes in the composition of the population
in old districts were used to advantage in allowing squares
to once more play a role in the process of social integration.
In redesigning old squares, the point is to find a balance
between the durability of the plan and to provide the area
with various forms of use.

OLD SQUARES

Noordplein

Submunicipality • NOORD
designer • dS+V, REINDERT VAN DER WAL
Artist • MICHAEL JACKLIN

Type of plan • SQUARE
Qualitative level • SELECT
Management level • INTENSIVE
Surface area • 12.000 m²
Date planning began • 1990
Date of completion • 1995 - 1996

Urban-Renewal Fund • F 150.000,-
Apportionment fund • F 461.000,-
City-council Priority 92/95 • F 1.000.000,-
General Fund • F 200.000,-
Nonmunicipal financing • F 200.000,-
Layout costs • F 167,-/m²

Situation in 1910.

Trial arrangement of tree lighting.

In the early 1900s, a steady increase in traffic on Hofplein led to the relocation of the vegetable market held there. A suitable site was found a short distance to the north, along the Rotte River, the supply route for market produce. A park in 'countryside' style, which was realized as part of Rose's canal plan, was situated next to a bridge between densely populated Crooswijk and the Oude Noorden. Vegetation was cleared away and the surface paved with clinker bricks. Rows of elms were planted to protect displayed vegetables from sunshine and rain. Noordplein, thus created, developed into a popular spot, where shops and cafés flourished. When road transport overtook the conveyance of goods by barges, the vegetable market disappeared from Noordplein, taking all activity with it. The only thing left, of any consequence, was cars. To prevent the square from being used as a parking lot, the municipality put up a forest of bollards and planters. These screened the already shady square from surrounding streets, leaving Noordplein a dark 'hole' rather than a connective route for pedestrians.

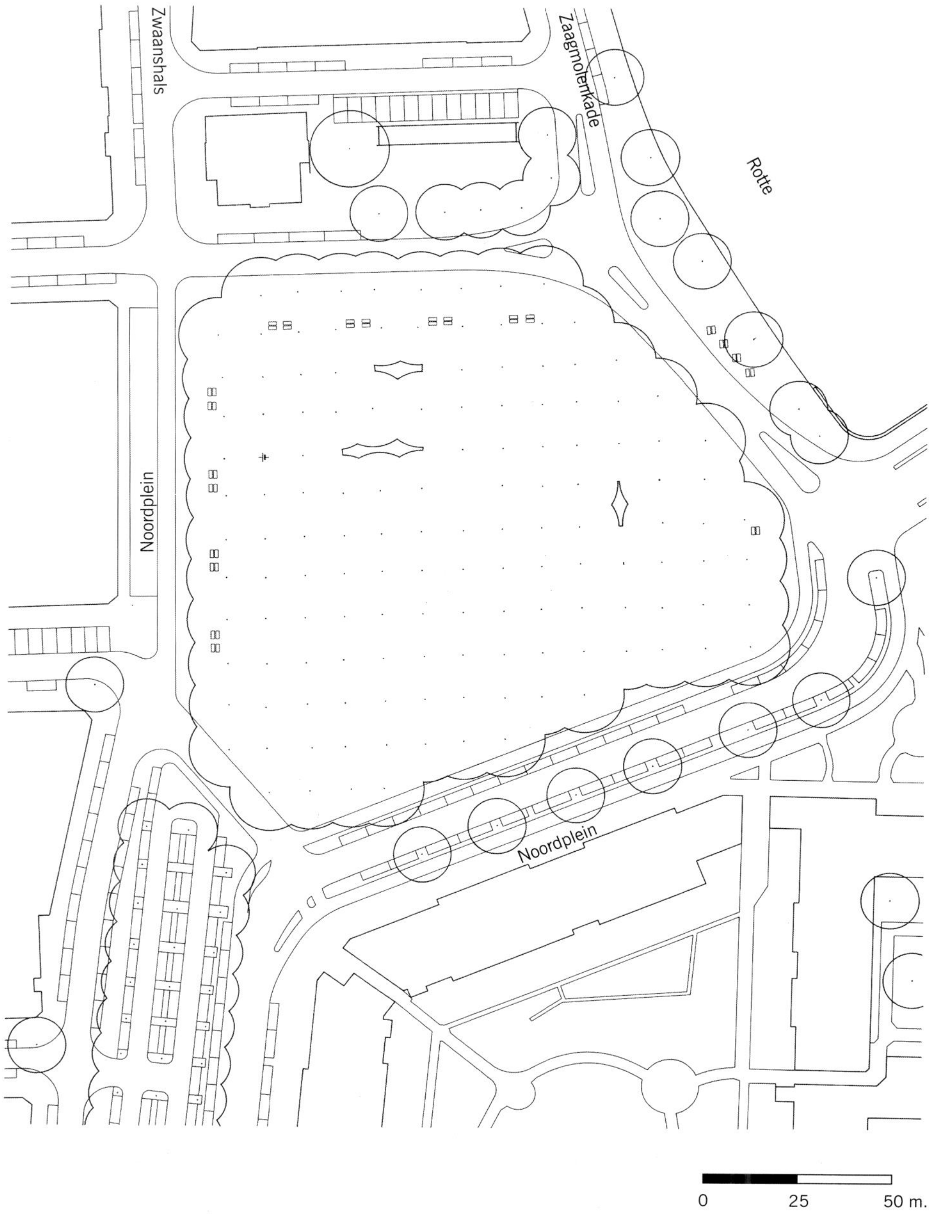

A discussion of this problem continued for a long time before a solution emerged on the horizon. Fortunately, proposals to chop down the trees have been rejected. The plan now being realized is based on the original surface design and the grid of elms. The threat of Dutch elm disease, however, may necessitate an adaptation of the plan. As long as the situation remains unclear, the plan is to remove all obstacles and thus create more light and a more unobstructed view. Floodlights mounted in the tree surrounds will illuminate the trees from below, and are meant to extend the cheerful appearance of the square even after sundown. Noordplein's attractiveness will be further enhanced when the street along its north side is converted into a broad pedestrian zone with places to eat and drink. Sidewalk cafés there will benefit from their location, midway between the shopping area and the mooring place of sightseeing boats on Rottekade. The success of Noordplein as an area for entertainment and urban events depends on keeping the square free of cars. For this purpose and as an experiment, a raised curb will surround the square.

Zwaanshals

Zaagmolenkade

Rotte

Noordplein

Noordplein

0   25   50 m.

Bospolderplein

Submunicipality • DELFSHAVEN

Designer • dS+V, ERIC NIJHUIS

Artist • DIET WIEGMAN

Type of plan • SQUARE

Qualitative level • SELECT

Management level • INTENSIVE

Surface area • 10.000 m²

Date planning began • 1993

Date of completion • 1994

Urban-Renewal Fund • F 1.900.000,-

City-council priority 92/92 • F 700.000,-

Layout costs • f. 260,-/m²

Situation in 1935.

Situation in 1961.

In 1982 urban renewal began in Bospolder. The only large area of open space in the district, the centrally located Bospolderplein, experienced drastic change. On three sides, the square is still bordered by existing facades and impressive plane trees, but the old school on the main side was torn down. The two housing blocks behind the school were consolidated into a new block accommodating housing for senior citizens. This new construction and the square's old layout, which was no longer attractive, made it necessary to renovate the square.

In 1986 Bospolderplein was one of the designs entered in the competition 'Three Squares, Six Designs.' Because of high maintenance costs, however, the winning design, created by Spanish architects Bach and Mora, could not be realized. To prevent the reorganization of Bospolderplein from becoming a long, drawn-out affair as a result of this abortive attempt, the decision was made to produce and realize an entirely new design for the square within a single year. All parties involved were invited to gather and to complete, as a team, the general layout created by a designer working for the municipality.

This layout consists of a broad, raised border surrounding large existing plane trees, playground equipment, and park benches. The border guarantees safety from traffic and, in addition, provides optimal accessibility, making it clear that the square is there for everyone. Broad steps next to the border lend access to a sunken, asphalt playing field, where visitors can play soccer and other games or just 'hang out.' Added to the square is an elevated section located in front of the housing for senior citizens; this pleasantly verdant area doubles as a buffer against noise pollution. Such a buffer is not superfluous, as conflicts abound among the various groups of users. The same area also accommodates a sculpture ensemble adjacent to several broad benches. Neighborhood children feel responsible for this work of art, because they collaborated with the artist in creating the concrete elements that compose it. Many benches are located throughout the square: beneath the 80-year-old plane trees, for those who want to sit in the shade or to catch their breath after a game of soccer; and in the green zone, for those who enjoy the sunshine, like to watch the children play, or, in the spring, find pleasure in the sight of bulbs, shrubs, and trees in bloom.

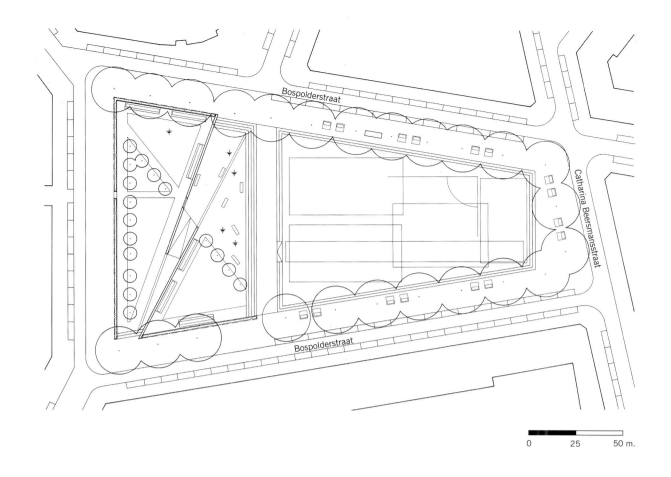

0　25　50 m.

129

Bloemhofplein

Submunicipality • FEIJENOORD
Designer • dS+V, ROLF CONSTANDSE

Type of plan • SQUARE
Qualitative level • SELECT
Management level • INTENSIVE
Surface area • 6265 m²
Date planning began • 1990
Date of completion • 1992

Urban-Renewal Fund • F 1.400.000,-
Layout costs streets • F 65,-/m²
Layout costs square • F 337,-/m²

Bloemhofplein is one of those squares that cannot be separated from the urban plan for the district. The Bloemenbuurt (Flower Neighborhood), which is part of the Bloemhof district, is divided by a cruciform of main streets, with the square at its center. Single-family, two-story dwellings under a pitched roof form a wall around the square, whose corners are marked by taller buildings. Originally, the square had a formal layout, which reinforced the appearance of adjacent development and fit into the garden-city atmosphere of Bloemhof. Rows of hornbeams, which lined both long and short sides of the square, composed a framework for public gardens crisscrossed by straight footpaths. Because of the need for more usable room, this ornamental layout was replaced in 1980 by two sports fields and a playground. The whole was provided with backstops and, to shield children at play from the traffic, shrubbery between the trees. These provisions made it impossible, however, to supervise activities from the windows of surrounding dwellings. The square deteriorated and became a place ignored by the

neighborhood. The residents' association needed all its resources, therefore, to convince those in the vicinity to support plans for a new design.
In order to restore Bloemhofplein's function as main neighborhood square, it had to become once more an area of open space, an area in which the intersecting axes would be discernible, in which people could meet one another, and around which they could live. Nothing of the existing layout was preserved. Trees in good condition were replanted elsewhere. A new transverse axis was designed; it functions as both footpath and meeting place. A canopy of treetops and areas of shrubs make the center of the square an intimate spot. On one side of the axis is an open field with facilities for ball sports for the older youth and, on the other side, a field with playground equipment for small children. The playing fields, in the form of plateaus, are about 40 cm above footpath level. This was a relatively inexpensive operation, since the original square was slightly convex. Parking places were moved to the residential side of the street. To tie the square into the urban context, once more rows of hornbeams were planted along the borders of the long sides and Italian poplars at the edges of the short sides.

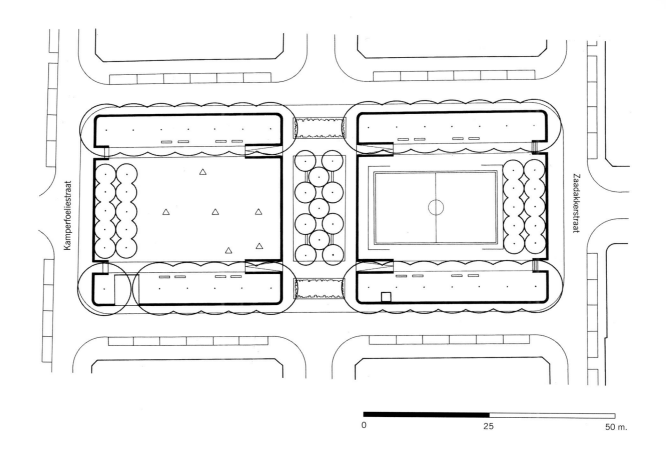

131

Virulyplein, 1994.

Beginning of Urban Renewal

'The reputation of Rotterdam's urban renewal extends far beyond our national borders. If you want to see urban renewal, you have to be in Rotterdam.' This was written, not without pride, by Pim Vermeulen, alderman for urban renewal, in the three-volume edition of *Stadsvernieuwing in Rotterdam 1974-1984*. In 1984, however, ten years of urban renewal were viewed not only with satisfaction but also with skepticism. There had been a great deal of good and affordable housing realized, but the appearance and use of redesigned streets, squares, and courtyards had failed completely to meet high expectations held by many. Much of this failure was due to the underestimated significance of open space within the urban-renewal process. Ever since

the view emerged that renovation of open space in existing districts requires an entirely different approach than renovation of the buildings themselves, necessary changes have been made in both planning and design of open space.

Run-Up to Urban Renewal

In the 1960s, municipal departments drew up a number of reports on how to handle the problem of run-down residential districts surrounding the modern city center. The *Housing-Improvement Report of 1969* stated that the municipality did not have to wait for sufficient replacement housing to be built elsewhere, but should begin with 'slum clearance' as soon as possible. Priority was given to demolition of neighborhoods lying along the trajectory of major infrastructural operations already planned. In deciding the order of other old urban areas to be renovated, the municipality waited for a structure plan that would include the entire city. In 1972 the first part of this plan was completed. In considering the development of Rotterdam, those formulating the report that included this plan based their ideas on a theoretical urban model in which the city center would accommodate only regional facilities and offices, and housing would be located along main public-transportation lines leading to the center. Although data on exact functions and surface areas were still unavailable, it was evident that the city was going to expand into areas occupied by the old districts.

Residents of these districts, who – already alarmed by housing-improvement reports – had set up action groups, protested in every way possible against threatening demolition operations and, in so doing, received support from leftist political parties. Their criticism was aimed not only at the removal of existing residential areas, but also at the idea of a city center with no housing function. They found the structure-plan report far removed from Rotterdam's real problems and developmental opportunities. All this commotion led to a political U-turn. In 1974 activities pertaining to the structure plan were discontinued, and the *Statute on Urban Renewal* was adopted. Public housing became the number one priority in the restructuring of old residential districts. A primary objective of the statute was a good home within a good housing environment, primarily for those in the lowest income bracket. An organization was established to lend shape to the new policy, and procedures were formulated. Each district had a project group for urban renewal. Chairmanship of these groups was held by a coordinator, who had direct access to the alderman responsible for urban renewal. Each project group drafted policy plans, plans pertaining to methods of approach, and development plans for its own district. In the decision-making process, the votes of residents' associations outweighed those of authorized officials 51 to 49. Any conflicts could be brought before the steering committee for urban renewal, composed of members of the Council Committee for Physical Planning, Transportation, and Public Works. Financial support for development plans was provided by the Interim Balance Regulation (IBR). This was replaced later by the Urban-Renewal Fund. Thus urban renewal was launched without a physical plan at the municipal level, which might have served as a framework. The new city council, whose members took office in 1974, expressed the need for a new structure plan in their integral policy report of 1975; such a plan would serve as a framework for urban renewal and as a document on which to base requests for subsidies from the central government. But the council had no wish to delay the active progress of the urban-renewal process. In advance of the structure plan, preconditions for urban renewal were formulated. These confirmed the importance of reinforcing the housing function in the city and of a decisive, pragmatic approach. At

that moment, open space was still a new area of policy-making. The council first introduced public verdure as a separate executive-committee portfolio in 1974. The Vermeulen Motion, which was made shortly after the integral policy report came out, asked for better coordination of housing improvement and housing environment. Development began on an open-space policy for the city, the main objective of which was to create more public space for recreational purposes.

The Initial, Experimental Phase

Prior to 1974, integrated physical-planning development did not exist within the Department of Urban Development. Open-space designers, planners, traffic engineers, and architects were not used to collaborating on a plan for an entire district or even on a neighborhood project. Although project groups introduced changes in this situation, an integral approach to public space was realized only to a certain degree. In every housing-environment study group, the open-space designer was responsible for producing plans for the layout of open space. Within the project group, responsibility for the development plan, and thus also for the location and dimensions of (new) areas of open space, was in the hands of urban planners. Besides the approach, the task of urban renewal itself – and all that it involved – was also new. There was no urban-planning or architectonic tradition behind the building of new housing in an existing neighborhood. There was no prior experience in the design of new areas of open space or in the layout of greenery within old districts. What did exist was an abundance of idealism and creativity. This was expressed in all facets of the urban-renewal process and most certainly in the design of the housing environment. The *woonerf* idea had just entered the scene, and streets due for major repairs were reorganized according to this idea, which included planters, ornamental railroad ties, playground equipment, and meandering routes for cars. Such projects were also carried out to improve living conditions while waiting for urban renewal operations to be realized. Consequently, further adaptations were often required after such operations had been completed. There were no objections: residents were customers, and the customer was always right, whether the request was for an extra balcony in the sun or a new shrubbery planter by the front door. The (necessary) construction of parking garages was intended to reduce the number of cars parked along the street and to replace them with flourishing communal activity.

Because public housing had high priority, the point of departure in formulating development plans was not, as a rule, the creation of the most desirable urban-planning structure for a neighborhood or district, but the architectonic quality of the dwellings themselves. Sometimes operations included a great deal of demolition, which made it possible to lay out squares at strategic spots, but the realization of a coherent system of streets, squares, and other open-space areas was not self-evident. In any case, demolition did not create a lot of space for extra verdure; of the total surface area made available by demolition, three-quarters was rebuilt. When the new structure plan of 1978 was issued, the sad lack of greenery in the old districts was mentioned once again, as was the general failure to eliminate this lack in the course of the urban-renewal process. The plan introduced no measures to correct the situation, however. Readers were referred to the green-matrix plan, which came out several months later. (The policy report *Green in Rotterdam* was adopted in 1979.) In the green-matrix plan, shortages of greenery in urban-renewal districts were supported by figures. An inventory of public space was carried out, and available recreational areas were rated according to WKWR standards, originally developed for green areas in new housing districts. Whether calculating the number of square meters of usable verdure for each resident or the walking distance to facilities at block, neighborhood, district, or borough level, the amount of verdure proved to be far below the norm. Within the system of priorities existing at the time (building, building, building), a claim for space in which to create larger facilities, such as district parks, was seen as unfeasible in the short term. An alternative was introduced: the concept of 'green veins' running throughout the city. By linking existing avenues, boulevards along canals, and strips of parkland to new, smaller elements, thus creating routes of verdure (green veins), existing parks and recreation areas farther away, outside the city, would become more easily accessible to residents of the old districts. A solution to the lack of verdure at block and neighborhood level was to be sought within development plans.

In practice, few changes occurred. Housing-environment plans continued to be designed and laid out for individual sections of individual streets, and lack of space nearly always prevented the creation of neighborhood parks. With the use of creative interventions and strategies, an effort *was* made to offer neighborhood residents, especially children, more green areas. One example is the 'claiming' of border zones. Pieces of land between districts were cleared and designed as parks or playgrounds. Another example is the opening of green courtyards to the public. Thus basic assumptions behind development plans, which led, in principle, to a lucid characterization of open space - streets as areas for traffic, squares as public gathering places, courtyards as the communal and private domain of residents - were not always carried through in building plans and project plans in a logical manner.

Large-Scale Production, Disappointing Results

In the early 1980s, housing production was going strong, and the urban-renewal train was thundering through Rotterdam's old districts, all of which led to a larger Verdure and Recreation Division. More and more often, open-space designers were needed to create housing-environment plans and thus to keep up the tempo of completed projects. Because the chronological order of urban-renewal operations was determined by the degree of urgency in tackling the 'slums,' urban-renewal districts became, as a whole, vast building sites. The dynamics of the housing process proved disastrous to the creation of open space. A realized section of a square was often broken up by construction traffic, defiled by building rubbish, and overrun by children practicing to be construction workers. It was virtually impossible to fully complete a housing-environment plan and to keep it tidy and intact. It seemed to be a waste of time and effort. In addition to the problematic nature of realizing projects in the midst of construction activities and daily life in the districts, completed streets, squares, gardens, and playgrounds were a disappointment. Public courtyards failed to satisfy preconditions for a peaceful, communal area and were hardly used. Streets designed as *woonerven* were unsafe because of the unclear division of areas meant for pedestrians and areas meant for cars. Nor did living along (busy) streets work in reality; living-room doors that open onto a street full of parked cars are rather inconvenient.

Another problem was the maintenance of the housing environment in urban-renewal districts. This consisted of nothing more than some extra sweeping and the care of plants, but even these measures fell short of expectations. Smaller facilities were used so intensively that they were often demolished soon after being completed. For those responsible for the greenery – people used to weeding and trimming, raking and mowing – the maintenance of planted areas surrounded by barbed wire, the endless replanting of damaged trees, and the removal of large quantities of litter amounted to a frustrating job. It began to dawn on those involved that the often complicated and vulnerable designs for residential open space had no chance of surviving the violent reality accompanying urban renewal.

In 1981 the partially revised *Structure Plan Within the Ruit* (beltway around the central urban area) acknowledged the importance of open space by making certain changes in the game rules of districts for which not everything had been set down in development plans. Instead of rebuilding three-quarters of the area made available by demolition, only half was to be required from that time on. This move increased opportunities for realizing squares and neighborhood parks. While the creation of more open space in urban-renewal districts was becoming a new policy spearhead, urban economy was weakening. The city council was forced to make significant cuts in the budget for management of public space; for maintenance of verdure, the cut was 30 percent.

The decrease in maintenance budgets had major consequences for the design of housing-environment plans in urban-renewal areas. In creating project plans, open-space designers were now forced to pay more attention to management costs. The necessity for restraint was translated into an aesthetic of clarity and simplicity. The shifting of axes in *woonerf* streets was 'rectified' by adding a sidewalk and a roadway, and by bringing back parking spaces. The new design credo, 'plain and functional,' was favorably expressed in the removal of an excess of 'sidewalk greenery' from the streets. It also led, however, to plans in which every frill was eliminated. Scrawny trees on new squares accentuated the bareness of their brick surfaces. Users found these minimally equipped open-space areas less attractive than earlier examples. Filthy conditions and vandalism increased. More and more, the image presented by urban-renewal operations was determined by the desolate state of streets and squares. Dissatisfaction with open space was common. It led to a motion introduced during a city-council meeting (the Verbeek Motion of 1985), in which a request was made for better management and maintenance of open space through the improved coordination or adaptation of its organization. Once again, the result was the establishment of an obligatory collaborative relationship, this time between three municipal departments: Public Works, Sports and Recreation, and Sanitation. Working Units for Public Open Space and District Maintenance Teams were established. Working Units were areas of operation limited in size so that Maintenance Teams could better carry out repair and maintenance activities and respond to complaints more rapidly.

Renewal of Urban Renewal

In calculating the balance of the first ten years of urban renewal, neglect of open space was recognized. In his foreword to the anniversary book on urban renewal, Alderman Vermeulen added to his words of pride: 'The building of thousands of dwellings where once were slums, while creating the prescribed housing density and following regulations and recommendations, cannot mask the loss of character found in streets and squares. Despite the relationship of its terminology to that of housecleaning, urban renewal is not a detergent.' There had to be another way to do things, but how? This question and others were discussed in what was, by then, a mature Verdure and Recreation Division of the Department of Urban Development, as well as in project groups. In 1986, such problems were tackled in a special urban-renewal workshop, in which people could collaborate on solutions to issues existing in all urban-renewal districts. An important conclusion was that the physical and functional coherence of open space at district, borough, and urban levels was in need of more attention.

With the appearance of an open-space designer as director of the Department of Urban Development, structural significance was finally granted to public open space as a discipline. The official organization was modified to such a degree that planners and open-space designers were included in one group, and collaboration among other divisions was streamlined. The urban-renewal process was also changed intrinsically. A method was developed for formulating policy plans for open space at the district level. These plans established the structure of the district as a whole and made a distinction between primary features – squares, main roads, and shopping streets – and minor matters. Policy plans for open space served as a basis for development plans and project plans. The results of such efforts were able to be

Pijnackerplein, 1970.

applied, in part, to the completion of districts surrounding the city center, known as first-ring areas, in which urban-renewal began. The final round of first-ring operations began in 1988. Together with reports entitled *Renewal of Rotterdam* and *The New Rotterdam* (1987), the *Renewal of Urban Renewal Report* was approved by the city council. The aim of this report was not a radical break with trends but a fundamental reassessment of policy. Key terms were housing differentiation, housing-environment differentiation, and rent differentiation. The building of good, low-rent housing remained an important goal, but the city, including the old districts, had to be made attractive to higher-income groups as well. Housing density in urban-renewal areas was to be reduced from 100 to 70 dwellings per hectare, and additional greenery was a must. And finally, the report argued for a rapid completion of first-ring districts. In Het Oude Westen, urban renewal came to a close with the successful reorganization of various streets and squares, which was based on a policy plan for open space. This instrument for open-space planning and the positive results produced in testing it here were of great importance to future urban renewal; the approach to the renovation of open space in second-ring districts, which was based on a similar policy plan, became the accepted procedure.

Het Oude Westen

OUDE WESTEN DISTRICT PARK

JOSEPHPLEIN

Het Oude Westen (The Old West) survived the bombardment of Rotterdam's inner city; the zoo in the northern part of the district was the only element completely destroyed. According to postwar urban-planning concepts, the barren plain that once accommodated the former inner city was to grow into a modern, functionalist city. These concepts allowed no room for Het Oude Westen, which failed to satisfy, all in all, the standards for residential districts being built on the urban periphery at that time. Right after the war, all physical-planning proposals made for the modernization and adaptation of Het Oude Westen were based on large-scale redevelopment and demolition operations. In 1964 such plans culminated in a proposal for phased demolition of the entire district, in order to make way for the new inner city.

In the early '70s, residents joined together to protest the plans and to demand that steps be taken to atone for years of neglect, dilapidation, and the deterioration of their housing environment. A special coalition included activists, designers, architects, and planners, who, dissatisfied with new, functionalist urban development, demanded the preservation and restoration of this lively, 'chaotic' urban district. In *Our Reconstruction Plan,* appreciation is shown for the heterogene-

ity and animated character of Het Oude Westen, which is presented as an exemplary form of urban living. In 1974 political recognition of this struggle for emancipation was formalized in the *Statute on Urban Renewal.* By socializing housing ownership and by preparing a development plan, nineteenth-century districts were to be restructured, and residents and planners were to fill in the rest in a relatively independent manner. For Het Oude Westen, this method of working resulted in the creation of a number of east-west breakthroughs that cut straight across the existing spatial structure of long, north-south streets; some of these breakthroughs were designed as a series of squares. Functionally, these new squares took on significance when facilities such as schools, health-care center, library, and supermarket were built next to them. Thus appeared a new spatial structure, which also supports a network of sociocultural facilities built to serve district residents in particular.

The attempt to preserve as many dwellings and job opportunities as possible in Het Oude Westen contradicted, however, the need for more public space. Enormous pressure came to bear on the design and use of the few open-space areas available. Some of these areas served more than one purpose: besides being neighborhood squares, Josephplein and Gerrit Sterkmanplein are also schoolyards. After many green and varied designs for squares and *woonerf*-like street layouts had failed, plans became austere and restrained; surfaces were usually of hard materials. The emphasis on building and renovating within the existing struc-

ture, wherever possible, prevented the creation of a large area of centrally located verdure. Space for a district park was made available only in 1987, when a large home for the elderly was torn down on West-Kruiskade. When the *Renewal of Urban Renewal Report* was approved by the city council, 76 percent of the housing in Het Oude Westen had been renovated. Of the open space realized, the only big success was the district park. Interest in open space, as called for in the report, reflects the change in thought concerning the approach to spatial structure. Where previously the focus had been on the building program and on the way in which projects fit into the architectonic fabric, now the chief aim was to realize a high-quality design of public space. A policy plan for open space was formulated, in which the district was seen as a spatially coherent whole. The general structure of open space was formulated and a typology of open-space areas defined. Schoolyards that doubled as neighborhood squares were provided with playground equipment. Long north-south streets were designed as traffic areas with parking places, and courtyards were laid out as quiet communal gardens or as private areas for residents of adjacent housing blocks. Realized according to special designs, many cross streets became pedestrian areas, which are linked to the squares. A number of plans for reorganization were carried out according to the new policy plan. Consequently, urban renewal in Het Oude Westen was able to satisfy the original objective: the creation of a lively urban district with a new spatial structure.

Het Oude Westen, situation in 1974.

Het Oude Westen, situation in 1994.

Zijdewindestraat, 1982.

BEGINNING OF URBAN RENEWAL

Oude Westen District Park

Borough • CITY-CENTER
Designer • dS+V, JAN HUIZER

Type of plan • PARK
Qualitative level • SELECT
Management level • INTENSIVE
Surface area • 17.000 m²
Date planning began • 1984
Date of completion • 1988

IBR-fund Oude Westen • F 1.263.000,-
Layout costs • F 74,-/m²

Oude Westen District Park is the last open-space project from the development plan of 1974 to be realized. District residents had to wait years for the demolition of the Simeon and Anna Home for the Elderly on West-Kruiskade. Only after this institution was torn down could the park be laid out. Drawing wisdom from experiences with squares and green courtyards, the residents' association recommended closing the park after dark and hiring a watchman to supervise the park during the day: a unique situation in Rotterdam.

Residents had high expectations of the park. They composed a detailed list of desired activities; at the same time, inspired by old trees gracing the garden of the former home, they imagined a romantic landscape. The designer was confronted with the task of producing a coherent plan for the available 1.5 hectares. The bare surface remaining after demolition, along with the intimate garden that had been preserved, suggested a park with a dual atmosphere, but one in which desired activities had a place. The formally laid-out northern section is for soccer and other games, sunbathing, and playing with pets. The informally laid-out southern area is fine for strolling, sitting on a bench to daydream, or enjoying the flowers. The linear construction of the

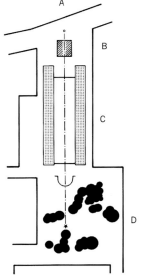

General structure
A. line of vision
B. quadrant of trees
C. tree-lined avenue
D. individual groups of trees

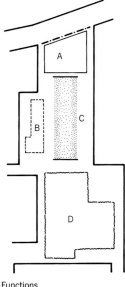

Functions
A. forecourt
B. small children's farm
C. sports field
D. romantic woods

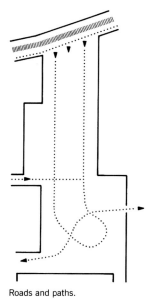

Roads and paths.

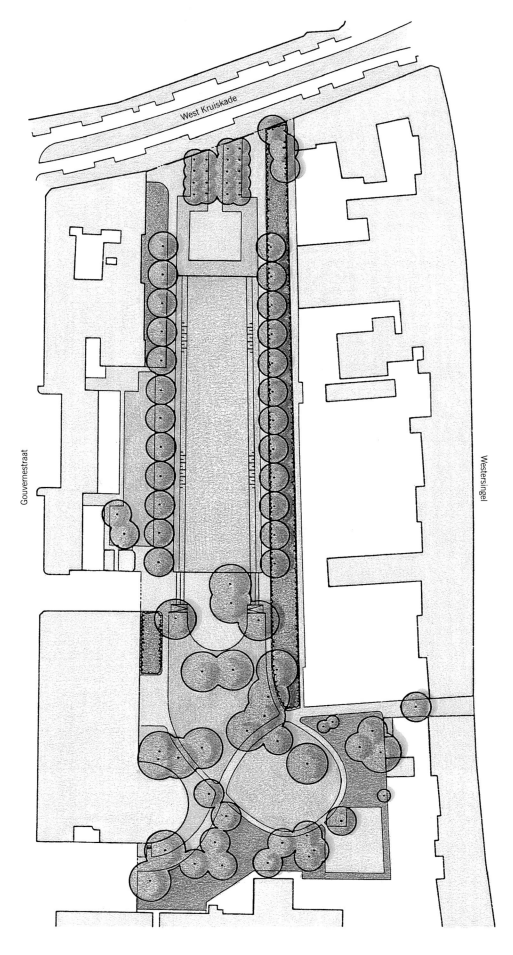

West Kruiskade

Gouvernestraat

Westersingel

0   25   50 m.

BEGINNING OF URBAN RENEWAL

park and the long lines of vision running through the central area create uniformity. The square directly behind the fence along West-Kruiskade forms a sort of balcony. Seen from the city, the lower-lying grass field and old trees are a 'natural' backdrop for benches and flower tubs on the square. Conversely, the square provides a transition between the busy shopping street and the peaceful atmosphere of the park.

Much of the value of a park within a densely built-up district lies in the experience of space. Because the park is bordered on three sides by the rear walls of apartment houses, the extraordinary view of the city across its vast lawns is all the more striking. Behind the richly detailed facades on West-Kruiskade, modern buildings on the Weena rise like abstract volumes into space. The intimate area in the informal part of the park is developing poorly, because many old trees have died and new ones are not thriving. Moreover, the planned breakthrough to Westersingel has not yet been realized.

Trees Oude Westen District Park

 1. Acer platanoides • Norway maple
 2. Acer pseudoplatanus 'Flavomarginatum' • Sycamore
 3. Aesculus hippocastanum • Horse chestnut
 4. Aesculus hippocastanum 'Baumannii' • Horse chestnut
 5. Ailanthus altissima • Tree of heaven
 6. Betula pendula • Birch
 7. Fagus sylvatica • Beech
 8. Fagus sylvatica 'Atropunicea' • Copper beach
 9. Fraxinus angustifolia 'Raywood' • Small leaved ash
10. Juglans regia • Walnut
11. Malus floribunda • Flowering crab apple
12. Platanus orientalis • Plane tree
13. Prunus subhirtella 'Autumnalis' • Winter flowering cherry
14. Pterocaria fraxinifolia • Wing nut
15. Pyrus calleryana 'Canticleer' • Ornamental pear
16. Quercus frainetto • Hungarian oak
17. Robinia pseudoacacia • Acacia
18. Sophora japonica • Japanese pagoda tree
19. Taxus baccata • Taxus
20. Tilia cordata • Small-leaved lime
21. Tilia platyphillos • Lime
22. Tilia europaea • Lime
23. Tilia europaea 'Koningslinde' • Lime
24. Tilia europaea 'Pallida' • Lime

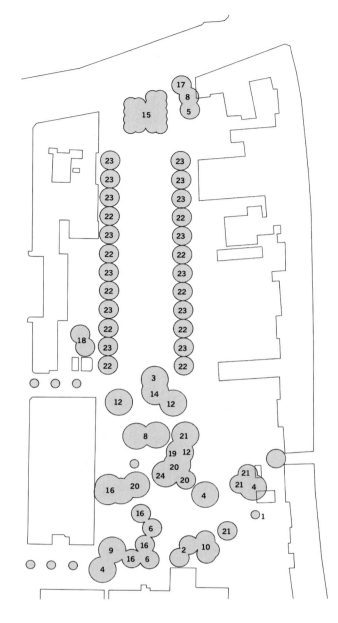

Josephplein

Borough • CITY-CENTER

Designer • dS+V, UWE SÖRENSEN, JAN ROOZENBEEK

Type of plan • SQUARE

Qualitative level • SELECT

Management level • INTENSIVE

Surface area • 3500 m²

Date planning began • 1989

Date of completion • 1991

Urban-Renewal Fund • F 435.000,-

Layout costs streets • F 65,-/m²

Layout costs square • F 167,-/m²

When urban renewal in Het Oude Westen was evaluated in 1988, the fact that squares appeared bare and neglected was acknowledged. Furnishings had proved to be unsatisfactory for usage requirements, and surfaces, which had been laid without preloading, displayed serious subsidence. Plans for reorganiza-

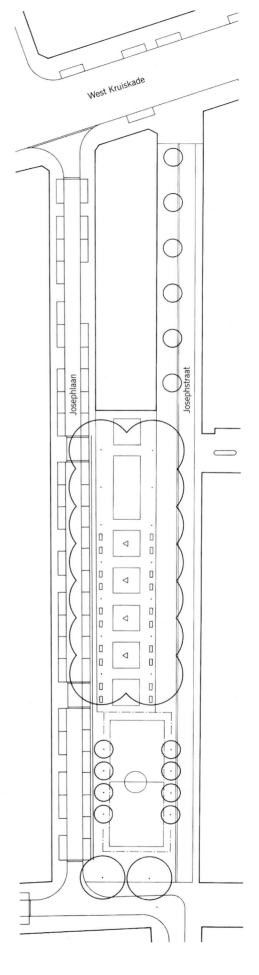

tion, which were based on the *Oude Westen Policy Plan for Public Open Space*, included a new concept for squares: blocks of verdure. The squares came into being after housing blocks were demolished. The latter were converted, with the use of trees, into attractive urban areas. One square reorganized according to this concept is Josephplein.

Coincidentally, a number of large plane trees on the Weena had to be removed to make way for the Plaza Complex. The Department of Public Works asked the project group of Het Oude Westen if these trees might find a new home on Josephplein. After being planted along former building lines of the narrow housing block now demolished, the trees fit perfectly into their new location. Originally, neighborhood residents and officials of the school bordering Josephplein displayed little interest in discussions on restructuring the square, but attitudes changed when funds were found for a

totally new design. The arrival of the trees was a festive, one might say spectacular, occasion: not only did overhead tram wires have to be detached from poles supporting them (which is why the trees arrived at night); all trees and lampposts had to be removed from Josephstraat as well.

To prevent cars from entering the new square, the surface of the border, in which the trees are planted, has been provided with strategically positioned benches, litter bins, playground equipment, and a chessboard table. The area within this border of relaxing activities is paved with a simple surface for sports and games. Residents permitted the relocation - but not the removal - of the existing soccer enclosure, the only successful element on the old square. Consequently, rows of plane trees do not surround the square in its entirety. Smaller trees have been used, however, to include the enclosure in the green area.

0   25   50 m.

Aelbrechtskade, 1995.

New-Style Urban Renewal

In the reports *The New Rotterdam* and *Renewal of Urban Renewal,* government expressed the desire to put less effort and money into inexpensive housing and to focus more on the creation of a complete city with an attractive and varied housing environment. This aim was already taking shape within the Department of Urban Development. Internal reorganization for the benefit of integral plan development and the approach to second-ring districts, based on policy plans for open space, had been fruitful. New project plans displayed far more coherence and identity. Experiments in Het Oude Westen had shown that the use of such a policy plan as a framework made it possible for those designing land-division layout and housing to design a square as well,

or for a playground to double as a schoolyard. In 1990 these innovations were included in a new administrative organization and in formal planning procedures; the Organization for Public Domain became the Organization for Public Open Space.

Once more, a motion made in a city-council meeting led to a new form of cooperation. The De Rijk Motion (1990) asked for a governmental decision on how to improve the quality of open-space planning. The answer was an integral planning process to coordinate activities carried out by various municipal departments; in addition, the term *quality,* used so often in reports, was defined and made operational. Of vital importance is a perception of open space as a coherent entity of buildings and (housing) environment and not as an appended facility. As a rule, (re)organization of open space does accompany building plans. The old planning process was modified to include these ideas. Originally consisting simply of design, realization, and management, it now has four or five phases: the initiatory phase (for all kinds of plans - even, for example, traffic-engineering interventions), the planning-team phase (only for building operations), the design-team phase (for planning open space), the realization phase, and the management phase.

From Initiative to Management

In the first phase of a planning process, the initiatory phase, the budget and a program of requirements for a project plan for open space are established by a management team consisting of the submunicipal official responsible for open space and project managers from Physical Planning, Traffic and Transportation, the City Development Corporation, and Public Works. Ideally, submunicipal policy plans for open space form a touchstone against which programs of requirements for project plans can be tested. Functions and desired levels of quality for open-space areas are, after all, already part of such policy plans. Generally speaking, urban-renewal areas fall into the 'standard' category. Only the most important structural elements of a district, such as central squares, main roads, and parks, are given special treatment. The initiatory phase is followed by the planning-team phase or the design-team phase, and sometimes by a combination of the two. According to the procedure, the planning team begins its activities before the design team is brought in, so that the two can collaborate in creating coherence between building plans and plans for open space. Permanent members of the open-space design team are a project manager from Public Works, a financial supervisor from the City Development Corporation, an administrator from the Rotterdam Recreation Division, and the open-space designer of the area in question. In certain cases, residents are represented in the design team by a delegation of residents' associations. When the open-space designer enters the process, open-space functions have been established, and the level of management the realized area will receive is known as well. Nevertheless, the design phase is a search for the significance of the site involved. Providing quality also means finding the correct solution to a problem and reinforcing the unique character of a certain spot and a certain district. If a reason exists and if funds are available, an artist can be called in to lend surplus value to a plan. The design team confers on rough drafts and coordinates all components of a plan. The design phase ends when the final draft is approved by all involved. This step includes checking the design to see if it satisfies each objective and condition set down in the program of requirements. The following phases – realization and management – include formal feedback to the design team. Realization, which is organized by Public Works, comes to an official end when the work is completed. The project is inspected by Public Works, normally outside the presence of the designer. Then begins the management phase, in which technical supervisors go to work. Technical supervision is not the only important aspect of the management phase; social supervision is vital as well. Many urban-renewal projects in the past were unsuccessful because residents did not feel an affinity with open-space areas. Scores of projects and events have been designed to encourage neighborhood residents, and especially the youth, to use and care for open space. Examples are *Opzoomeren, Duimdrop,* and *Bonkers.* On Opzoomer Day, residents clean public areas together and, in so doing, earn items such as benches, planters, and playground equipment, to be used where they see fit. The Duimdrop project involves the distribution of containers of toys on squares and plazas. By behaving well and doing small tasks, children can earn play money with which to borrow objects from the containers. Evidently, after this program started, children who were hanging around with nothing to do or who were causing trouble started having fun playing together outdoors again. Bonkers is a project in Het Oude Westen, organized by the residents themselves. Young people follow a course to become 'playtime supervisors' and are then asked to lead children's activities.

Only after a design has functioned within the community for awhile can its success be determined. The evaluation of a project is an important moment. If elements of a design have not worked as expected, the error has to be remedied. Funds must be reserved for this purpose. The impossibility of correcting mistakes was a big urban-renewal problem in the early 1980s. Although there were budgets for new squares and parks, money for reorganization was nonexistent. Street renovation, a maintenance tool that had always formed a relatively inexpensive way to alter poorly functioning designs, was lost in the sea of retrenchment. Another reason for a lack of management funds was the failure of Public Works to include in the budget additional costs for damage caused by vandalism. The management system views vandalism as a phenomenon too unpredictable to have norms applied to it.

The New Planning Process in Practice

The new Organization for Public Open Space has been operating since 1990. In the beginning, administration always took place at the central urban level, and teams were chaired by coordinators of open space from the Physical-Planning, Traffic, and Transportation Division of the Department of Urban Planning and Public Housing. In anticipation of the autonomy of submunicipalities in 1997, however, decentralization is now taking place. Submunicipalities are responsible for organizing the planning process and monitoring the progress of projects; more and more often, both planning and design teams serving urban-renewal projects are chaired by a submunicipal policy-making official or management coordinator. Thus the formal organization of the design and management of open space in urban-renewal operations has undergone an essential change. Political re-

Duimdrop on Bospolderplein.

May 28, 1994: Opzoomer Day in Rotterdam.

sponsibility has shifted to submunicipalities and now lies, therefore, much closer to the users. Designers, technical supervisors, recreation experts, financial authorities, and other specialists function as advisers to submunicipal administrators and residents. Expected was that an organization with such clear-cut rules and such direct lines of communication would overcome predicaments that once hindered urban-renewal plans for open space. In practice, however, the process is not that simple. When problems need an explanation, participants in the game frequently blame one another.

Residents and their representatives find that in many cases designers and, to a lesser degree, technical supervisors, still gaze down at open space from their ivory towers. From such a height, they fail to see what is happening in the districts. In the battle between various groups of users for scarce space, mountains can be made out of molehills. A seesaw can mark the boundary between territories belonging to older children and tiny tots. Designers are blamed for not looking deeply enough into information about social processes that result in projects such as Duimdrop and Bonkers. They are also blamed for not showing interest in initiatives, developed by the residents themselves, that relate to the design and management of open space, such as Opzoomeren. The Rotterdam Recreation Division complains, too, that designers look only at form, and that they fail to use information available from the RRD on activities of various age groups or on the suitability of different kinds of playground equipment.

Designers, however, claim that they are often forced to act as referees. When users' groups are intolerant of one another, a designer often feels obligated to support weaker interest groups. These are, in particular, the children, who do not attend resident-participation meetings, and groups less used to standing up for their interests during exchanges of ideas at the district level. The designers of the Department of Physical Planning, Traffic and Transportation blame residents for being unable to make decisions when certain usage requests can not be combined. And they accuse submunicipal administrators of being lazy: the latter too often blame conflict situations on the design and are easily tempted to score points by proposing simple material solutions for problems put forward by residents. Tension exists at all times between, on the one hand, the money and attention available for the larger necessities, central facilities, and structural elements of a district, and, on the other hand, the money and attention demanded by residents for the streets on which they live. Under pressure from residents or other interest groups, administrators do not always honor their commitments to quality. Furthermore, according to designers, their plans are not well implemented, realized projects deviate from their drawings, and there is a lack of technical supervision. When, after years of consultation, a carefully designed open-space project is finally realized, but poorly, the result has little to do with quality. Thus, in the eyes of the open-space designer, it is usually the technical supervisors who are at fault when realization or maintenance of open space leads to vandalism.

On the other hand, technical supervisors claim that designers go to work with too little functional knowledge and come up, time after time, with plans for square wheels. They blame designers for their insufficient understanding of demographic developments and of related, quantitative recreational needs within a given district. Moreover, they complain that opting for special materials means that when something is in need of repair, it takes longer to get the correct replacement materials and thus longer to remedy the situation. Large quantities of expensive materials cannot be kept in stock and often have long delivery times. A situation in which every District Maintenance Team has all sorts of materials and maintains all constructions optimally is impossible to organize and to finance. Therefore, when an exclusive design for a square receives only temporary repairs, the designer, who felt compelled to create something original, is to blame. The efficiency of maintenance is seen similarly: designers often fail to remember that maintenance is tied to budgets and that a complicated system of logistics is involved.

The conclusion to be drawn from all these complaints is that the planning process is open to improvement. The design procedure is, in principle, well-organized. Many of the design team's disagreements on project plans could be prevented if the management team were to resolve controversial issues in the program of requirements, as well as other conflicting interests. The design may not be used as a shovel to scoop hot coals out of the fire. In commissioning projects, too often submunicipalities still act as clients instead of as administrators. It is wrong to consider the design complete simply because the working drawing has been prepared and approved. The design is finished only when it has been implemented down to the last detail as agreed, or, in other words, according to drawings and specifications. A good idea is to include the designers in the realization process. Even if they do not actually supervise operations, they should at least make an occasional inspection tour of the site and pass on their thoughts to those in charge. The job should be considered done only when, following a final inspection, the project is given the designer's seal of approval. The management procedure also lacks competent organization. It can be improved if, as a hard-and-fast rule, funds are reserved for evaluation and possible adaptation. When technical supervisors add their signatures to a design, thinking, 'We'll figure out a way to maintain it,' and the realized project turns out to be difficult to maintain, the only solution is a structural one.

Together, design, implementation, and management form a continuous cycle. By arranging evaluation sessions, by compiling and recording information on developments within districts and neighborhoods, and by making this information available to administrators, designers, and managers, funded projects, which adapt the housing environment to the needs of the residents, can be realized, time after time. The composition of the population in urban-renewal areas is often subject to powerful dynamics, and, in many cases, it is difficult to predict how a certain spot is going to be used. When the planning of open space is seen as a public-private partnership, all participants in the planning process must make an effort to appreciate both the others' positions and the interests shared by all. The existence of such an attitude will lead to the creation of worthwhile areas of public open space in Rotterdam.

Berkelplein

Submunicipality • KRALINGEN/CROOSWIJK

Designer • dS+V, WIEBE OOSTERHOFF

Artist • BAS MATERS

Type of plan • SQUARE

Qualitative level • SELECT

Management level • INTENSIVE

Surface area • 4620 m²

Date planning began • 1984

Date of completion • 1989

Urban-Renewal Fund • F 428.000,-

Layout costs streets • F 65,-/m²

Layout costs square • F 120,-/m²

The problem with the district of Jaffa is that it lacks an identity of its own. There are no special elements, and its urban-renewal facades are architectonically boring. People living in the new dwellings have extremely diverse origins.
The objective of the new square is to create an attractive space that invites the presence of a variety of functions and expresses a community feeling. In short,

the square is to become Jaffa's 'living room.' Although the area is almost square and is adjacent to a symmetrical building, the design is not formal. If the square is to be part of life in the district, interest lies not in an imaginary axis drawn from a building, but in how the area is used. And this use is linked to functions surrounding the square and to routes through the district. The community center and the Turkish Society are diagonally opposite to each other. The line between the two is part of the route children take to go to the nearby school. The design is based on

this diagonal. The richly contrasting elements conjure up a private world within the square. The most noticeable feature is the sculpture, which can be interpreted in various ways. Against the curved wall seat, the high table with bowl is a symbol of life together in the district; against the backdrop of trees, it can be seen as a bower, a little house in which to take shelter. But the work of art is also a singular object, consisting of two triangular volumes, which together form a star and which seem to move, as the spectator moves, in relation to each other.

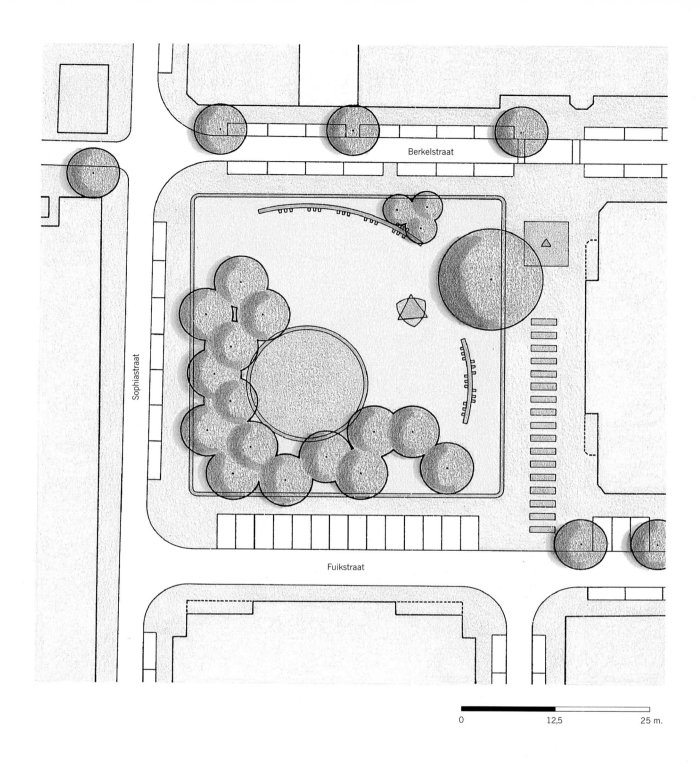

Berkelstraat

Sophiastraat

Fuikstraat

0   12,5   25 m.

Next to the symbolic sculpture, a recessed circle of smooth, red asphalt forms an element quite suitable for outdoor recreation. Children can use it for roller-skating, playing marbles, or putting on plays. It can function as a wading pool in the summer and as an ice-skating rink in the winter. Berkelplein's square, yellow, paved surface lies within the original building lines. Because this surface is not directly connected to the street, beneath which lies a network of cables and pipes, it remains unaffected by street repairs. Noteworthy is the temporary layout, which previewed the definitive design, that Berkelplein was given during the year that its bedding of sand underwent preloading. The diagonals consisted of wood-chip-covered paths between stairs at the corners. Tree trunks, adorned with little flags attached to them by schoolchildren, served as trees. The circle was covered with wood chips as well, and a refreshment stand stood at the spot that would later accommodate the sculpture. A plan of activities assured that the preloading period, instead of resulting in a sandy fiasco, became a time of anticipation. Residents were able to claim the square as their own even before it existed.

Technical data

To prevent expected subsidence, the site experienced one year of preloading. For this purpose, the site was raised with a layer of sand approximately 2.00 m thick. To shorten the hydrodynamic period, vertical drainage, which reached a depth of about 14.00 m below Amsterdam ordnance datum was used. This process made use of plastic drains, which, placed

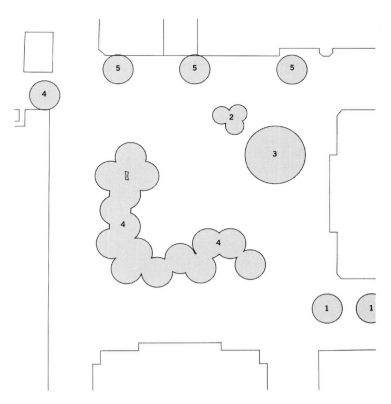

at intervals of 1.75 m in triangular relation to one another, were distributed throughout the site. In addition, horizontal drainage was used to remove surplus water and to maintain the existing ground-water level throughout the preloading period.
At the end of one year, subsidence was approximately 1.15 m. Following this preloading period, a layer of sand measuring 0.40 m was removed. Remaining subsidence has been calculated to measure between 0.40 and 0.50 m over a period of 25 years.

Trees Berkelplein

1. Carpinus betulus 'Fastigiata' • Fastigiate hornbeam
2. Carpinus betulus 'Frans Fontaine' • Hornbeam
3. Populus euramericana • Poplar
4. Robinia pseudoacacia 'Casque Rouge' • Acacia
5. Sorbus aucuparia • Mountain ash

Kasteeltuin Spangen

Submunicipality • DELFSHAVEN
Designer • dS+V, COR GELUK

Type of plan • PARK
Qualitative level • SELECT
Management level • INTENSIVE
Surface area • 18.000 m²
Date planning began • 1987
Date of completion • 1992

Urban-Renewal Fund • F 1.950.000,-
Layout costs • F 108,-/m²

The Kasteel, home to Dutch soccer club Sparta, is a stadium located on a unique site in the district of Spangen. Plans are in the works to offer the club new accommodations outside the district. In anticipation of this move, the training field on the west side of the stadium has assumed the role of a park. Residents requested a

park with a neat appearance and various functional possibilities.

A square on the south side of the park forms a connection to the district. The prominent arcade on the square assures that the park, still young and filled with immature vegetation, does not get lost against the volume of the stadium. As time passes, the visual function of the arcade – as a tall, massive object – can be assumed by trees in the park. Placing an avenue along the wall of the stadium was also done with future modifications in mind. The avenue forms a border of trees

that softens the view of the wall and offers room for playground equipment. In the future, it can evolve into a self-evident spatial axis. On the north side, the park's location next to the beltway, along a bend known as the Spaanse Bocht, has been used to advantage. This highway follows the curve of a canal and of a railroad line for freight. Shrubbery planted along the border of the park does not obstruct the view of the densely vegetated railroad embankment and of solitary trees lining the watercourse. Standing in this 'illusion' of a larger park,

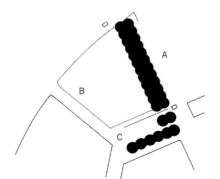

Major elements:
A. mature trees
B. fencing
C. pergola

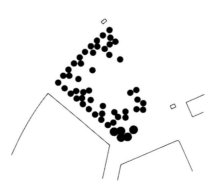

Young vegetation.

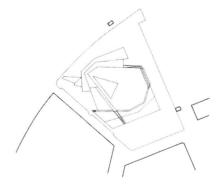

Texture of the surface level.

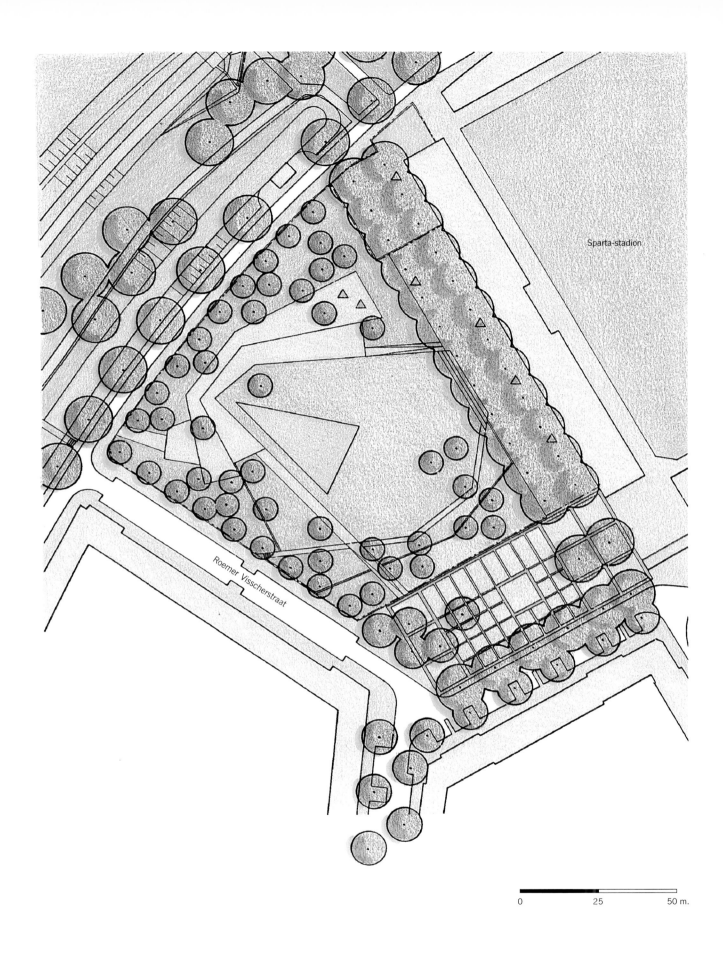

Sparta-stadion

Roemer Visscherstraat

0   25   50 m.

NEW-STYLE URBAN RENEWAL

the visitor is reminded of romantic parks in which long views play significant roles. The choice of rhododendrons and shrub roses for border vegetation has a dual significance: they are suitable for a park and, at the same time, transform the periphery into a lushly blooming border, which lends the small park the character of a large garden. The name of the park, which means castle garden, was aptly chosen.

The park is well-anchored into its surroundings and can allow itself, therefore, to assume a certain degree of introver-

sion. The park turns inward by means of terraces that begin along the border and slope down to a triangular pond in the middle. Despite minor differences in level, artificial relief renders a powerfully spatial effect. This relief is provided by a variety of ground-level textures – grass, gravel, low shrubbery – and by pale curbing around the terraces, which creates neat, geometrically shaped areas. Path surfaces are of crushed dolomite, a gravel-like byproduct of stone-quarry operations. To create differentiation in the paths, both a fine and a coarse composi-

tion of crushed dolomite were used. The fine type compresses well, but the coarse type remains loose and granular and is not as easily negotiable for visitors unsteady on their feet, those using wheelchairs, and people with baby carriages. The material ended up in the grass, with annoying consequences for lawn mowers, and even in the pond, where it was thrown by children. The problem was solved by removing the coarse dolomite gravel, mixing it with a finer composition, returning it to the paths, and compressing it.

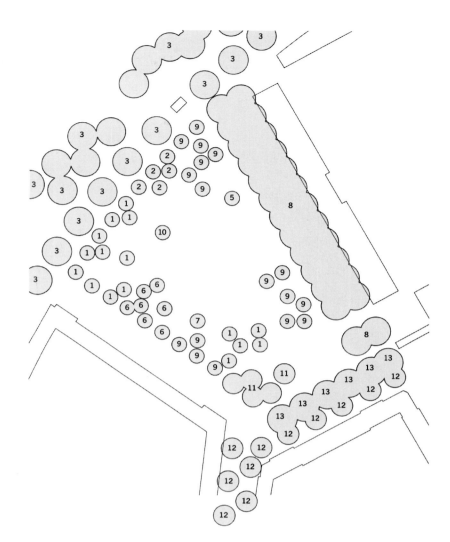

Trees Kasteeltuin Spangen

1. Corylus colurna • Hazel
2. Fraxinus angustifolia 'Raywood' • Small-leaved ash
3. Fraxinus exelcior • Ash
4. Liquidambar styraciflua • Sweet gum
5. Magnolia kobus • Star magnolia
6. Malus tschonoskii • Flowering crab apple
7. Paulownia tomentosa • Fox glove tree
8. Platanus acerifolia • Plane tree
9. Prunus avium 'Plena' • Wild cherry
10. Pterocarya fraxinifolia • Wing nut
11. Quercus frainetto • Hongarian oak
12. Robinia pseudoacacia 'Bessoniana' • Acacia
13. Ulmus hollandica • Elm

Tweebosdwars

Submunicipality • FEIJENOORD
Designer • dS+V, EELCO GEILL

Type of plan • HOUSING ENVIRONMENT
Qualitative level • SELECT
Management level • INTENSIVE
Surface area • 16.000 m²
Date planning began • 1991
Date of completion • 1993

Urban-Renewal Fund • F 3.200.000,-
Layout costs streets • F 65,-/m²
Layout costs square • F 287,-/m²

Afrikaanderwijk is one of the districts in Rotterdam South that were once home to a great many dockworkers. Its neighborhoods are characterized by plain perimeter blocks and long, straight streets. The Tweebosdwars project is one of the district's last major urban-renewal projects. It is the result of intensive collaboration among residents, architect, urban planner, and landscape architect. The project covers the area, which once accommodated two long housing blocks, between De la Reystraat and

Afrikaanderplein. The former wall of facades along Afrikaanderplein was replaced by four apartment towers, which correspond in height to other recent high-rise development along the park. Residents in the neighborhood behind the towers can see and reach the park through the area that separates the towers. The long perimeter block between Christiaan de Wetstraat and De la Reystraat was replaced by two short housing blocks, which function as an intermediate element between high-rise development and older buildings. The new, small cross street is linked to an existing pedestrian route that runs straight through the Tweebos neighborhood.

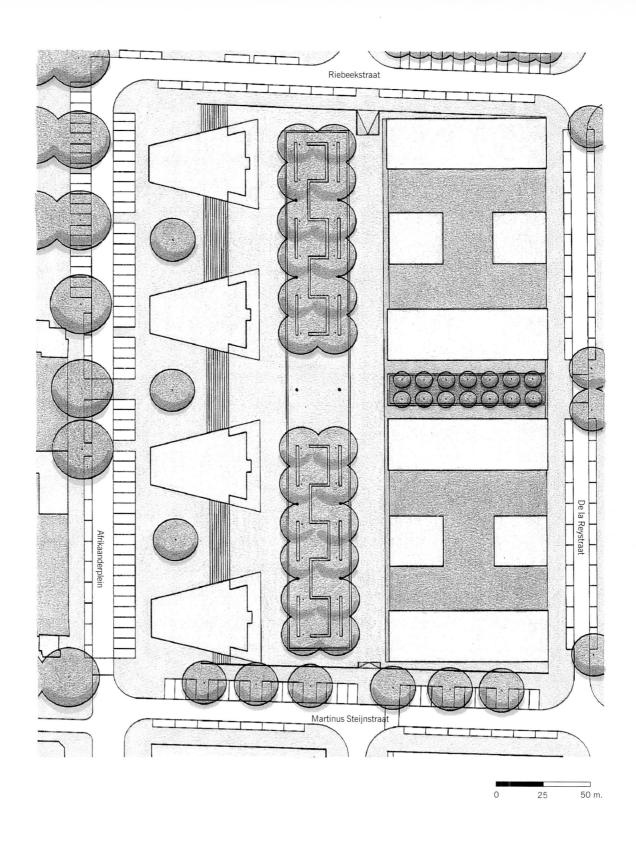

Riebeekstraat

Afrikaanderplein

De la Reystraat

Martinus Steijnstraat

0   25   50 m.

Designing the new building volumes was difficult because of the uneven surface of the site, which slopes in a diagonal direction down to Afrikaanderplein. The problem was solved by situating all construction at one level and by spanning uneven areas with stairways and retaining walls. This solution also lent a strong sense of uniformity to the planned area. This approach provided Christiaan de Wetstraat with a new function. This elevated and broadened 'street' is no longer a thoroughfare, with parking spaces for cars, but a connection for slow-moving traffic and a pleasant outdoor area for residents in adjacent housing. Entrances to the towers are also situated here.

Because the park is nearby, and because there are many playgrounds in the vicinity of Tweebosdwars, residents thought it would be a good idea to provide this area with a layout and furnishings geared to (older) residents who want to spend quiet time outdoors.
A meandering white line on the paved surface connects a series of 'little rooms': intimate spaces with walls consisting of low, trimmed hedges and with corners marked by trees. By day, the 'rooms' get sufficient natural light. In the evening, they are illuminated by outdoor lighting resembling floor lamps.
Benches and litter bins complete the picture.

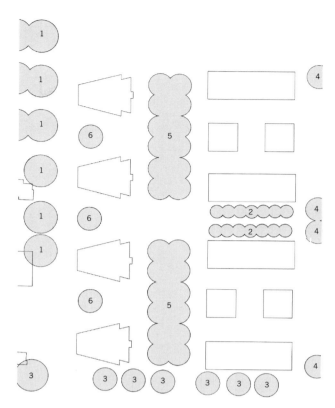

Trees Tweebosdwars

1. Platanus acerifolia • Plane tree
2. Robinia pseudoacacia 'Umbraculifera' • Acacia
3. Robinia pseudoacacia 'Bessoniana' • Acacia
4. Sorbus aucuparia 'Fastigiata' • Mountain ash
5. Tilia tomentosa 'Brabant' • Silver lime
6. Corylus colurna • Hazel

NEW-STYLE URBAN RENEWAL

Tidemanplein

Submunicipality • DELFSHAVEN
Designer • dS+V, RIA AARNINK
Artist • MARGIT RIJNAARDS

Type of plan • SQUIARE
Qualitative level • SELECT
Management level • INTENSIVE
Surface area • 16.000 m²
Date planning began • 1986
Date of completion • 1993

Urban-Renewal Fund • F 735.000,-
Layout costs streets • F 65,-/m²
Layout costs square • F 142,-/m²

The layout of streets in Het Nieuwe Westen is based on a combination of land divided into *slagen* and a symmetrical composition. Formerly, an elementary school was at the center of the district, but it lacked an accompanying schoolyard. Within the framework of urban renewal, the school was assimilated into a new block, and part of the existing block was demolished. As a result of these operations, a square was created: the new heart of the neighborhood. A new community center built against the side of the former block forms an extra, functional impetus. The square serves as playground for both district and school. This dual function prompted a great deal of discussion on the design and management of the square. School officials wanted the square to be related, as much as possible, to the school building. The residents' association was afraid that soccer-playing youth would take over the square, leaving few playground opportunities for younger children and little room for community-center activities. A clever design distributed the available space among the various users, giving each group its own area without dividing the square into separate 'territories.'

Problematic was the considerable difference in height between Tidemanstraat and Van Oosterzeestraat. In designing the square, this problem was solved by laying out the entire surface of the square, which lies within boundaries formed by old building lines, at the level of community center and school. A low fence accentuates the autonomy of the elevated square and shields the playground area from traffic. The plan is based on the theory that 'form follows function, and function follows form.' The central area has an asphalt surface. Because it is also free of obstacles, it is optimally suited for ball games and activities 'on wheels.' Borders were paved and provided with benches, trees, and playground equip-

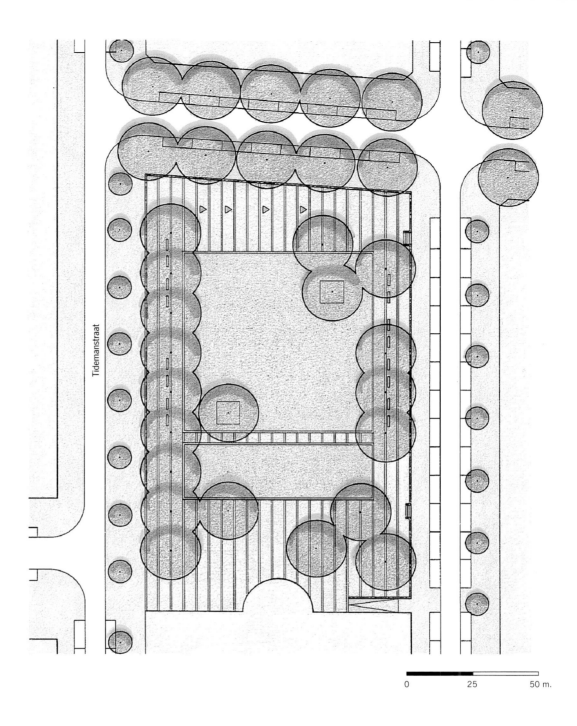

Tidemanstraat

0   25   50 m.

ment, furnishings that do not encourage rough behavior, but which invite small children to relax and enjoy themselves. The community center has an area of its own in front of its entrance. A 'platform' protects the area from soccer games and is, at the same time, an element linking both parts of the square. It accommodates playtime activities and can be used as a stage during festive events. The floor of the platform is a smooth, black, rectangular surface bearing an abstract, graphic design.

Technical data
Preparation and realization of the design revealed the need for a number of skillful maneuvers to compensate for consider-

able differences in height between streets surrounding the square. To achieve a perfectly horizontal site, the decision was made to situate the future square at the level of the highest street and to use a retaining wall with stairs to make up the difference in height between this and the lowest street level.

Because most of the square was to lie on land formerly occupied by gardens belonging to demolished housing, an area that had never supported any weight to speak of, there was real danger of subsidence. To prevent extreme subsidence, a preloading period of nine months, using a layer of sand 1.50 m thick, preceded the realization phase. The square could not be situated at the lowest street level

because the ground-water level there is too high.

The platform design entered the scene at a later date. This element was to stand 40 cm above the surface of the square. A geological-engineering study showed that the platform needed the support of piling, since it was outside the area that had undergone preloading operations.

On the square, young acacias (size 20-25) rise above steel tree grids (with a grid opening of 33 mm) surrounded by concrete curbing. Tree stakes have been deliberately set into the concrete and not within the tree surrounds, so that the grids provide the surrounds with maximum coverage. A porous cloth beneath the grid discourages the growth of weeds.

'Every borough can go ahead and develop its own bollard'

A discussion with Nico Kamphorst, the alderman responsible for public open space in Amsterdam borough of De Baarsjes, and Lex Brans, project manager of Mercatorplein and surroundings, also in De Baarsjes

'ACCORDING TO ME, A TENSE RELATIONSHIP EXISTS all over between what Physical Planning hands out and what Public Works realizes. The best model is a model that makes sure that these two participants collaborate as closely as possible. Decentralization in Amsterdam has evolved to such an extent that it's possible for a submunicipality to develop an autonomous policy on public space. Every borough can go ahead and develop its own bollard and tree surround. We do that too. Management of thoroughfares takes place according to agreements between the appropriate members of councils from boroughs adjacent to those thoroughfares. Traffic affairs are directed by the city council, but the details are left to us.'

'Relationships within open-space management are another story. We have our own sanitation department and open-space maintenance crew. We operate with a comprehensive budget, which also covers borough management. The budget is based on maintenance standards drawn up by municipal departments. There's always a difference between what we want to do and the amount of available resources. Furthermore, it's easier to let a street wait for a year and to renovate a school building. Fortunately, the Urban-Renewal Fund is available to us. We can draw money from that for public space. We realize that this fund allows us to do things now that are no longer possible in other parts of town and that won't always be possible here either. To tell the truth, we haven't yet decided what we're going to do when urban-renewal budgets dry up.'

'We've used the opportunity to set relatively ambitious, high-quality goals. Our basic principle is: plain and functional. But at strategic spots, such as Mercatorplein, Surinameplein, and Hoofdweg, we're trying to do a little more. For this purpose, we established a Monumental-Aspects-of-Public-Open-Space Fund, a separate budget for street furniture and the like, to supplement the budget for standard furnishings. Such structures have existed within the field of public housing for a long time, but not within the area of public open space. The basic standard for spatial quality is stated in the Policy Plan for Public Open Space. Right now, we're in the process of deciding which facilities and materials to use to lend substance to this extra opportunity for quality. 'Plans for open space are, in fact, a public affair. For this reason, we involve residents as much as possible. This process begins with a survey during the preparatory phase, continues in the form of presentation and participation meetings, and includes other activities for the distribution of information. All this is necessary, but sometimes a big problem as well. Experience has taught us to draw a clear line, as soon as possible, between those matters that can be influenced by residents and those over which they have little or no influence. When these rules have been established, the game can be played correctly. I've found that, under these conditions, the qualitative criteria we draw up don't have to differ that much from what residents want. Occasionally you see a discrepancy between what designers envision and what residents have in mind. In such cases, as an administrator, I pay very serious attention to the people who have to live there. Spatial quality that goes unrecognized by users is, in my opinion, an empty ambition.'

'We are conscious of the fact that we have to deal very carefully with walls of facades and with street profiles in Berlage's plan. We're trying to maintain, as well as we can, the uniformity of execution that typifies the urban plan. But you also have to realize that we're not working in an open-air museum. Since the '20-'40 beltway was developed, its function has experienced drastic change. In the past, neighborhoods around the beltway were on the urban periphery. Old photographs attest to streetscapes now extinct: a grocer's cart, groups of children playing. Today, main bus and metro lines make their way through these districts, which are also confronted with morning, noon, and evening rush-hour traffic. In addition, we're dealing with an extremely varied composition of the population, from which highly diverse requirements and priorities emerge. Everyone would like very much to have safe, clean streets and squares. We're using two different methods to meet this demand. We've now assembled, under one roof, all borough-level departments that deal with management, maintenance, and security. This is leading to more concerted cooperation and to accelerated procedures. In addition, we've introduced a kind of spring-cleaning operation, in which every street gets a triennial overhaul. Together with residents and landlords, we examine the condition of street furniture, assess unsafe spots, note overdue maintenance of greenery and the like, after which the whole street is restored to tiptop shape.'

'Ever since Amsterdam was subdivided into boroughs, reorganization of plans for public space has become a complicated business. Continual negotiations with municipal departments are vital, to persuade them to help pay for renovations. Their attitude is usually one of procrastination or refusal, because their plans for major repairs on tramlines or the sewage system, for example, are out of sync with our reorganization program. Such plans are jealously guarded secrets. It is becoming increasingly important to keep up with the level of administration on which, and the department by which, a project is initiated; this initiator is then the actuator of the work, the party with the most responsibility, which leads others to adopt a kind of hitchhiking attitude.'

'In the case of the Mercatorplein project, we are, in essence, the party behind the operation: we're commissioning the design of its new layout and we're making funds available. The project is based on a form of public-private partnership. The work is to be carried out, wherever possible, by certified companies. This means that activities will be subjected to continual quality-control inspections. Central municipal departments and services don't have such a system. So there's no upsurge in efficiency in that area. The technical condition of facilities determines whether or not something needs to be improved or replaced, not the internal or external market or a need for integral spatial quality. Within this context, conducting business in a coherent manner isn't easy. Starting in 1998, we'll assume responsibility for the complete urban administration of our borough and will be able, therefore, to enter into contracts with then-autonomous municipal departments. The integration that we're now attempting to implement in the Mercatorplein project will then become standard throughout the entire borough. My advice to other Randstad municipalities who are reorganizing would be to get your own departments in order as quickly as possible so that you can correlate policy and management at an early stage. Under such circumstances, innovations get a much better start.'

'In the case of ordinary projects in De Baarsjes, budgets for planning, realization, and management have to be directly coordinated. Our approach to the Mercatorplein project is more broadly based. Here private parties – such as shopkeepers and landlords – are involved in the investment in, and management of, public space by means of long-term taxation based on area improvement. Such taxes are paid in addition to normal property taxes. After all, the interested parties most involved shouldn't mind paying extra for a higher level of quality. A general agreement among all involved – municipality, borough, and private parties – includes provisions for cooperative activities in the areas of management and maintenance. These long-term agreements need to be developed in more detail for the management of housing, as well as for the maintenance of public space. As governmental administrators, you must be prepared to guarantee that your part of the agreement will continue to be actively upheld. Such a guarantee carries with it the vital importance of administrative continuity. We've been able to make financial agreements – valid up to 1998 – with the central municipal government on the allocation of budgets. If this hadn't been successful, private parties wouldn't have participated.'

'We consider ourselves lucky to be part of the second and third generation of urban-renewal operations. So far, we haven't fallen victim to the dialectics of progress. We're learning a great deal from completed projects in Amsterdam. Urban renewal in the Netherlands began with housing. The early '70s saw the implementation of extravagant renovation projects, in which the only urban-planning criterion applied was the preservation of old building lines. As a result of this sectoral definition of aims, six months after certain districts in Amsterdam had been renovated, front doors were falling off their hinges. Another lesson gained by experience was that public space also requires improvement and that landlords and residents need to be persuaded to take their part of the responsibility for such areas. Such ideas were expressed in taxation based on area improvement, for example, but also in concrete initiatives on our part, such as involving the local population in a tree-planting project.'

'At the moment, we're about halfway through the realization program. If subsidies cease to exist in 2002, I wholeheartedly hope that we will have finished the job. Otherwise we have a big problem here. It's true, De Baarsjes will be an autonomous municipality by then, and we'll have the chance to generate our own revenues, but in the context of a people's district like this one, that's still not so easy. We hope that we won't soon be forced to say: "Unfortunately, a project like Mercatorplein is no longer possible."'

Workscapes

The Port and Industrial Area

For years the design of open space was no more than an insignificant feature of land-granting and infrastructural projects. Part of the reason is that – compared with public space in the city – publicly accessible open space in port and industrial areas is in relatively short supply. Land is allocated in parcels of many hectares, sometimes dozens at one time. Public space is concentrated around infrastructural elements. The policy was to plant as many trees and shrubs as possible.

In order to create an integrated policy on open space in the port area, the Rotterdam Port Authority drew up the *Rotterdam Structural Concept for Open Space in the Port Area* in 1993. This concept states that public open space can contribute

significantly to an attractive business environment, on the one hand, and, on the other, to a pleasant outdoor environment in the port area and immediate vicinity. The aim of the structural concept is to promote a harmonious development of public open space by specifying the direction such development is to take in the port area. The concept is not 'a plan to be implemented,' but a touchstone containing preconditions and basic principles for all projects in the port that are related, even indirectly, to the planning of open space. Desired development has three main objectives: an improved relationship between the port and its surroundings, elucidation of the composition of Rotterdam's port and industrial area, and the accentuation of the port's unique character.

165

An Improved Relationship Between Port and Surroundings

The first objective of the *Rotterdam Structural Concept for Open Space in the Port Area* is an improved relationship between the port and its urban and rural surroundings. Down through the centuries, this relationship has experienced radical change. Originally, port and city were inextricably bound together. Port activities took place on the river, in the heart of the city. Over the course of the twentieth century, the port expanded in the direction of the sea, causing a separation between city and port.

This seaward expansion, which stemmed from a great need for new, large-scale sites, occurred mainly on the left bank of the Maas. Toward the end of the expansion period, in the 1970s, the oldest harbor basins in the urban area were dismantled and taken over by urban functions. Port functions in such close proximity to (advancing) urban functions became increasingly problematic. Furthermore, because of their size, the (inadequate) depth of their basins, and their (in)accessibility, old harbor sites became less and less suitable for port activities. From an economic viewpoint, of course, city and port remain interwoven. The shipping exchange is located in the city, many dock industries have their offices there, and berths for barges and other inland vessels are also found in the city. Transshipment, however, has disappeared from the heart of the city. The harbor triangle Leuvehaven-Wijnhaven-Oude Haven is now the recreational Waterstad (Water City), and the Kop van Zuid project is being realized on the left bank of the Maas.

During the period of westward expansion, transition zones between the port and its surroundings were designed to alleviate as many problems as possible between the two domains. On Vierhavensstraat, the border between port and city consists of a principal dike, a street, a switchyard, and abundant verdure. The border between port and countryside is formed by National Highway 15, which, at certain places, creates the impression of a wooded area. South of this highway lies the Hartelkanaal (Hartel Canal), with behind it a water-recreation zone – Brielse Meer and Oostvoornse Meer (lakes) – and beyond this zone the rural area of Voorne Putten. To the north are the port areas of Botlek and Europoort, which are largely hidden from sight by trees and boscages.

The aforementioned visual separation between port and rural area is understandable. In rural surroundings, the transition between the old agrarian landscape and industrial sites can be brutal: the large scale of a tank park versus the small scale of a historical residential area such as Brielle. The transition zone softens contrasts while, at the same time, it limits the nuisance factor for the surroundings, such as the inconvenience of noise, dust, and stench. Within the urban environment, 'wrapping the port in green' is not as suitable. On the contrary, the task here is to create a 'port front' on the border between port and city. Obviously, the nuisance factor attached to harbor activities must be kept to a mini-

Plan of the port area
1. Waalhaven
2. Eemhaven
3. Petroleum Harbors
4. Botlek
5. Europoort
6. Maas Plain
7. Europahaven
8. National Highway 15/railroad line
9. Eemhaven Distripark
10. Botlek Distripark
11. Maasvlakte Distripark
12. Brielse Meer
13. Oostvoornse Meer
14. Oostvoornse Dunes
15. Voorne-Putten
16. Hook of Holland
17. Midden-Delfland

mum, but the activities themselves do not have to be hidden. After all, Rotterdam is proud to be a seaport.

The visitor should be given the opportunity to experience the port not only along urban boundaries of harbor areas, but also within those areas themselves. The structural concept for open space makes no open attempt to stimulate this recreational joint use – traffic jams can prove disastrous to the economic functioning of the area – but it *is* willing to direct such use, by means of the Dutch AA Port Route, for example. To aid the display of port, water, ships, and transshipment activities, the structural concept designates areas in which vegetation is to be removed and sites from which panoramas can be viewed by visitors. In addition, several 'old-fashioned' opportunities for recreational joint use are mentioned, which include activities in green areas south of Europoort and along the beach bordering Maas Plain. Finally, thanks to its expanse, the port area currently offers temporary accommodations to several noisy, space-guzzling recreational functions, such as a shooting range and a cross-country track for bikers.

Elucidation of the Composition of Rotterdam's Port and Industrial Area

The second objective of the *Rotterdam Structural Concept for Open Space in the Port Area* is the elucidation of the composition of Rotterdam's port and industrial area. Harbor sites from east to west differ quite a bit in function, layout, fur-

nishings, and spatial character. Such differences are related to the current and former function(s) of the site in question and to the stage in which transshipment technology found itself at the time of realization.

Older harbors consist of rather narrow sites fronted by very long quays, originally meant for the small-scale transshipment of general cargo and bulk goods such as grain and coal. Examples are Maashaven, Waalhaven, and Merwehaven. Goods are stored indoors, as a rule, previously in warehouses and currently in (refrigerated) storehouses and silos, making the size of eastern harbors comparable to the size of urban areas. Harbors built more recently were created to accommodate bigger ships, industry of a more extensive nature, and large-scale transshipment of bulk goods and containers. Examples are the Petroleum Harbors in Botlek and Europoort, and the Europahaven on Maas Plain. Goods in these western harbors are stored in a more 'open' manner, allowing their physical character to be defined as wide-open space, across which various elements, such as factory installations and storage tanks, appear to be strewn.

The structural concept for open space tackles reinforcement of the spatial structure of the port area by focusing on the main infrastructural entity: National Highway 15 (also called Europaweg here) and the railroad line serving the port. This route transports both business and recreational visitors along the various harbor sites. The idea is to create a 200-meter-wide *scenic portway*, consisting of highway, railroad

Neckarhaven, Europoort.

Seinehaven mole, Botlek Distripark.

tracks, underground network of cables and pipes, service road, and unused areas. In laying out and furnishing this strip and the immediate vicinity, extra attention is being paid to street furniture, vegetation, signage, management, lighting, the inclusion of small-scale industrial sites, orientation points, and the appearance of industrial sites bordering the *scenic portway*. This part of the port is seen as the showpiece of the area.

Accentuation of the Port's Unique Character

The final objective of the *Rotterdam Structural Concept for Open Space in the Port Area* is the accentuation of the unique character of the port. The aim is to develop and reinforce the identity of the portscape by means of design and architecture, and by the way in which the functions of verdure and scenic beauty are handled. For years the use of verdure has been *the* way in which to achieve spatial quality; such use gave greenery a visual-aesthetic function. Trees, chiefly poplars, and shrubs were planted with the intention of either dressing up public space or concealing industrial sites behind a 'screen of green.' According to the structural concept, verdure should add an element of structure to the landscape and should designate entrances to industrial sites, public highways, and recreational areas.

Opportunities for the use of verdure in eastern harbor areas, however, are limited. The density of development is relatively high, while the majority of public space is filled with above- and underground infrastructure. Since roads have to be wide enough to accommodate trucks, since berms have to remain open to satisfy traffic-safety requirements, and since strips containing networks of cables and pipes may not be exposed to root growth, many places are suitable for nothing but grass. On western harbor sites – Botlek, Europoort, and Maas Plain – possibilities for the use of verdure are greater. 'Natural joint use' can even be found here. These sites are part of the coastal area. They are expansive, with a sandy soil composition, salt water, and an open landscape, which is highly influenced by sea winds and sunshine. Within this area are many spots that remain undeveloped for economic reasons: unused sites given in option to companies located nearby, strategic reserves, strips containing cables and pipes, land between storage tanks in tank parks, and residual zones too small or too poorly situated to be of any use. These areas – rarely visited by humans, but abounding in birds – are home to pioneer vegetation consisting of beach grass and dune scrub.

The emerging thought is that these harbor areas need no additional verdure and that extensive management of natural vegetation will suffice. The total area of open sites remains approximately the same, but sites not in use at any given time are occasionally found in different locations. These dynamics cause few problems, ecologically speaking. It does make sense, however, to calculate the degree to which it is necessary to leave sites undeveloped within the port area to serve as 'stepping stones,' or 'corridors,' between ecological systems north and south of the port: Hook of Holland, Midden-Delfland and the Oostvoornse Dunes. The second aspect determining the identity of the port area is found in architecture and design. This aspect is primarily functional; the term 'design' is not used in the classic-aesthetic sense. The urban-planning structure is, for the most part, nautically determined: waterways and harbor basins are situated to ensure safe and efficient shipping activities. In addition, this structure reflects the logistic process: the layout and furnishing of terminals, routes linking container terminals with Railroad and Inland-Navigation Service Centers (where containers are loaded onto trains and barges), and the highway network.

The design of buildings and objects within the port area has been handled in the same functional manner. Storage tanks, storehouses, petrochemical installations, silos, and transshipment cranes are built according to a specific functional logic. Furthermore, most offices situated throughout the port are devoted to terminal, storage, or distribution activities. The port area contains no large-scale office sites; port industries receive their clients and other business relations at headquarters located in the city. For this reason, little attention is paid to creating a distinguished appearance for office buildings in the port itself.

Distriparks assume a special role within Rotterdam's port and industrial area. (Such parks are found in Eemhaven and Botlek, and one is scheduled for realization on the Maas Plain.) These are relatively small-scale industrial sites linked to National Highway 15 (Europaweg) and used for distribution activities. Direct contact with clients occurs frequently here, and this can be seen in the special spatial quality that exists in distriparks. Plans for the development of individual buildings elsewhere in the port area barely take into consideration regulations governing lines of vision, building lines, building volumes, and so forth. When the distriparks were developed, deliberate use was made of such regulatory tools. The structural concept for open space underlines the importance of paying more attention to aesthetic aspects; at the same time, however, it aims to protect the identity of the port, which is characterized by its functional, robust design. All things considered, the solution to problems of design in the port area lies in the hands of the restrained creator, who will approach the utilitarian character of the port area with respect.

Beach next to the Maas Plain Oil Terminal.

Maas Plain.

Distripark Eemhaven

The 'snake wall'.

The nearly 65 hectares accommodating Distripark Eemhaven are located as close as possible to this container harbor, on a site just south of National Highway 15. This location meant that large-scale port activities had to be fit into the existing small-scale landscape of Albrandswaard North. In addition, designers had to keep

in mind the future disappearance of the polder landscape's agrarian function. An attempt was made to achieve a high-quality spatial design. The connection to the areas of Waalhaven and Eemhaven, as well as to Highway 15, is formed by a striking overpass. A comprehensive plan made for this distripark integrated the urban arrangement of the industrial buildings, the handling of traffic, and the layout of open space. The distripark has a simple layout with three patterns of development. The size of two strips, north and south, is geared to the storage of goods, also known as warehousing. A central strip accommodates joint-cargo activities: the handling of containers and their contents. The shielding zone is an important element in a distripark. Its main functions are to soften the view of the industrial buildings for those in the surrounding countryside and to muffle the noise that accompanies port activities. The design of this zone uses a series of artificial hills in elongated pyramidal forms. The diagonal lines of these volumes engage in play with the horizontal and vertical lines of the storehouses. The Koedood, an existing watercourse next to the highway, was shifted to the foot of inclines to the south and was broadened here and there to create large ponds, along which runs a route for cyclists and pedestrians. Green, sound-damping screens made of wickerwork with a steel core are positioned on the lower inclines and at the narrowest places in the shielding zone. One spot, which required higher sound-damping screens, was provided with a 'snake wall' designed by landscape architect and artist Krijn Giesen. The wall consists of a winding steel cage that contains rubbish produced by the demolition of local housing and accompanying vegetation. The history of the area has been accumulated and condensed, as it were, into a new border line. The wall seems to be a monument to demolition, but it does not merely represent decay; it is also evolving. In the future, all sorts of wild plants will take root on the wall, and birds, bats, and other small creatures will have occasion to find shelter here.

Spaanse Polder business site, 1993.

Green Business Sites

'Rotterdam, Working City,' 'No Words, Just Action,' 'Rolled-Up Sleeves', 'Gotta Git Workin": these are just a few of the slogans that characterize Rotterdam in both a positive and a negative sense. Such expressions were fueled by the enormous task facing Rotterdam at the end of World War II: both port and flattened inner city needed to be restored and expanded. This challenge was accepted.

The bombardment of the inner city eradicated a multifunctional area, which included as many as 3,450 companies. A decision was made to relocate these companies to industrial sites outside the city center, rather than to restore the original premises. The most important area created to receive this new development was the Spaanse Polder, the

largest single-function working area outside the port. The Spaanse Polder lies north of Rotterdam, between the Schie and the Delfshavense Schie. Postwar reconstruction of companies was accompanied in most cases by a substantial increase in scale. Moreover, good accessibility for inland vessels was high in priority. For this purpose, a series of harbor basins was realized along the Schie for the transshipment of raw materials and other goods.

In laying out and equipping industrial sites, efficiency was number one. Space available for industrial sites was developed. Although residential districts that housed employees were expected to be provided with verdure and were carefully designed, any beautification of working areas was considered ridiculous, an attitude easily understood in the context of the postwar era. Seen in this light, it is amazing that an industrial site such as Waalhaven South was provided with a green central area, an exception that was to remain so for a long time. Gradually, however, the demands companies made of business and industrial sites began to change. With the increase in road transport, the importance of accessibility via waterways for economic activities outside the port diminished, and more weight was given to accessibility over land and to the presence of space for parking. The proximity of a good connection to the nearest highway became a particularly significant factor.

Differentiation of Companies, Sites, and Open Space

During this same period, important shifts in Rotterdam's economic structure were taking place. More firms from the commercial and service branches of industry began appearing alongside the traditional manufacturing companies. This broadening of the economic structure led to a need for other types of sites and for more specific kinds of spatial settings. Industrial sites were frequently referred to as business sites. The desire not to lose those organizations looking for something other than the usual industrial or business site and, in addition, the desire to attract new companies, launched a discussion in Rotterdam on the quality of business sites.
The development of the business park Rotterdam Noord-West illustrates revitalization in plan development. The plan originally developed for this area was considered a high-quality product by the planners involved. Like residential districts of the '70s and '80s, the plan had an informal character. The irregular pattern of streets even included a cul-de-sac. Verdure was to consist of abundant masses of vegetation, which were to articulate the site and to present a green appearance to those approaching the premises. The area was to be accessed by the main highway running through the Spaanse Polder. The plan failed to make an impression on the market, however. Even after part of the street plan had already been realized, not one potential candidate had shown any interest in the park. Obviously, something was wrong, but what? To find out, members of the business community already established in other business parks were interviewed. This survey revealed that the layout of the new site was unacceptable to potential tenants. Those interviewed criticized the park's inadequate accessibility, in particular: only one access point and no direct access to the highway going north. In addition, they found the network of streets a maze, the subdivision inefficient, and the vegetation inappropriately situated. Greenery in front of their business premises was unwanted; facades and company logo had to remain visible. On the other hand, they liked the idea of verdure along the main access route, since greenery here would contribute to the attractiveness of the area as a whole.
In a collaborative effort, municipal departments then developed another concept, which included the market demands of those interviewed. This plan is now in the final stages of

realization. A precondition requiring companies to have their buildings face main, verdure-lined access streets has resulted in a combined presentational effect: this effect is achieved individually, by means of well-designed buildings, and collectively, by means of well-planned open space. Based on experiences in planning Noord-West and on a growing insight into what companies want, a typology of business sites has been developed. Differentiation in patterns of requirements has been translated into a series of ten different business environments, which includes everything from inner-city office boulevards and companies located in residential districts to large-scale business sites in and beyond the port area.
The diverse business environments are distinguished by differences in planning factors (subdivision, appearance, infrastructure, degree of functional blending, building shapes), as well as by various factors based on the surroundings (proximity to: highway, public-transportation station, port, shopping facilities, outlet area). A translation of market demands plays a central role. Subsequently, based on the abovementioned series of business environments in Rotterdam, three spatial-economic clusters of business sites have been distinguished. The southern cluster, on the left bank of the Maas, finds itself in a harbor atmosphere. Businesses opting for this cluster are more interested in a strategic location between port and hinterland and in a good infrastructure than they are in ambience. The northwestern cluster, which includes the business park Rotterdam Noord-West, is geared to all sorts of organizations oriented toward the Randstad. The eastern cluster, with its urban atmosphere, includes the districts of Kralingen and Prinsenland, the Kralingse Lake, and Erasmus University. This cluster is attractive to businesses looking for an environment that reflects their own high quality; just as firms in Noord-West, their marketing area covers the Randstad. The eastern cluster offers a good location to those in the service industry, among others.

The First Step Toward Green Business Sites

In realizing a business site, the philosophy of coherence among target group, site, and design gave rise to a concept for the development of a high-quality site on a special spot in the eastern cluster. The location, between Erasmus University and the highway, appeared to be exceptionally suitable for smaller offices 'with an identity of their own' – a category very much in need of such facilities in the mid-'80s – and for high-quality firms presenting an office-like appearance. The site was well-suited to accommodate university-related organizations as well. The idea was to create a new working environment in a park-like setting. The project would respond to the express wish for distinguished surroundings to accommodate corresponding businesses. The park-like setting was to be accentuated by placing several ponds in the central area and by using a staggered building line. Furthermore, as many buildings as possible were to be visible from the highway, fulfilling an-

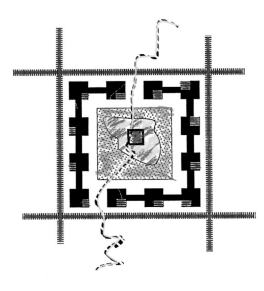

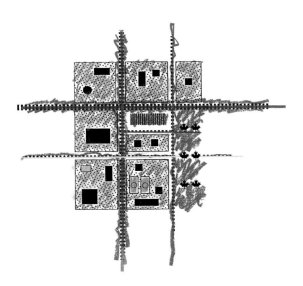

Models for green business sites:
Working green.

Campus.

other request made by the business community. The site would be made complete by a spacious, green layout. Thus was Brainpark 'born.' The concept proved to be a first step in realizing a green business site. The site's outward appearance, especially as seen from the highway, gives little impression of verdure, however. To begin with, as many buildings as possible were situated along the highway, and second, the market demand for individual 'charisma' was overindulged. As a result, such individuality, as realized on the outside edges of the site, certainly does not present an image of quality, and verdure realized within Brainpark has a decidedly inward orientation. A concession was also made in the inner area, which now accommodates three large office buildings instead of the two originally planned. Fortunately, this was the only concession made. The projected, good-sized ponds were realized, and the side of the area facing inward does have a park-like appearance. The layout of vegetation, also that of private premises, was very carefully supervised. At that time, it was innovative to subject the design of private plots of land to the approval of the municipality, which wanted, in this way, to avoid an incoherent green matrix and an individual layout of gardens. Maintenance was also uniformly coordinated.

The Future of Green Business Sites

Rotterdam still faces an enormous task when it comes to the development of business sites. The region has an annual demand for 50 hectares on which to build business premises. The existing supply is small and does not fulfill the requirements of all types of businesses. On the one hand, there is an urgent need for new sites; on the other, space is scarce, and there are many other claims to be honored. In addition to space for business sites, space is also required for residential areas, recreation, agriculture, and, not to be

forgotten, the natural environment. It is logical, therefore, that in the field of physical planning, the rather forced planning of clustered functions is increasingly seen as objectionable. Integration of 'green,' 'red,' and 'purple' on planning maps could result in environments of a higher quality. Combining housing and working areas within green surroundings and fitting businesses into scenic green matrices are planning concepts arising from such thinking. For the latter concept, a better term than business sites might be 'workscapes.'

There are still other advantages tied to green business sites. A noticeable trend is the increasing amount of importance that companies are placing on surroundings with a pleasant ambience. Green business sites can play into this trend and thus contribute to the further differentiation of business environments. An interesting development would be the replacement of individual charisma, still highly coveted by many firms, with beautifully laid-out, green business sites. This development has already occurred outside the Netherlands. Cambridge Park and Stockley Park, to name two English examples, are the proof. In a certain sense, Sophia Antipolis, on the French Riviera, can also be seen as such. Furthermore, green business sites can also be used to reinforce the regional green matrix. The Rotterdam region has relatively few attractive scenic and cultural areas of landscape; to use these as business sites is socially unacceptable. By linking the development of business sites to (pre)investment in the landscape, both the number of hectares of green space and the number of hectares of business sites can perhaps be increased considerably.

Green business sites and workscapes can play a role in Rotterdam's urbanization areas both north and south of the Maas. To the north, expectations are that the northwestern cluster and the eastern cluster will fuse into a single north-

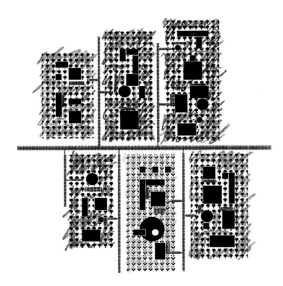

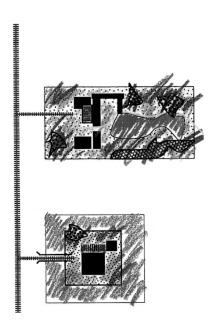

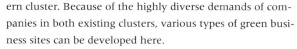

Working woods.

Estate.

ern cluster. Because of the highly diverse demands of companies in both existing clusters, various types of green business sites can be developed here.

A survey of potential green planning concepts revealed four different possibilities. Of these, the 'working green' is nearest to being the continuation of an existing green business site: the first Brainpark. The new plan does place a more decided emphasis on vegetation, however. The working green, which might be located on the urban periphery, has a primarily office-like character. This may prove particularly interesting to entrepreneurs north of the Maas.

The 'campus' is a type in which housing and business premises are integrated within a green environment bearing a recognizable, urban identity. Campuses of technological universities in Delft and Enschede serve as references. This concept is of special interest to the northern cluster. The campus might form a transitional environment between single-function residential areas and working areas or might border a recreation area.

The 'estate' is an exclusive type that probably will not be realized very often but that offers interesting opportunities for the development of areas of scenic beauty and those of ecological value. Because it is attractive to discriminating businesses, it fits especially well into the northern cluster, whose marketing area covers the Randstad.

The fourth type, 'working woods,' is especially appropriate for the southern half of the conurbation. Although companies in the southern cluster have less need of visibility and charisma, this is the very area in which afforestation might lead to more space for businesses. In using woodland for business sites, the intention is to plant the trees well in advance of preparing the business sites; such a plan assures that sites are actually in the woods after trees have been chopped down to make way for them. This concept also

offers flexible opportunities for organizations to expand over the course of time.

Development of green business sites is currently in the early stages, and a number of judicial snags still plague the various planning concepts. For example, present physical-planning regulations do not allow for the acquisition of land to be used temporarily as woodland and, at some future date, for the joint function of woodland-business site. Moreover, joint functions are financially complicated as well. Creative structures and strategies will be needed. And ultimately, the business community itself will have to find the animo to invest in the development of sites imbued with scenic and spatial quality. In any case, somebody out there is going to capitalize on trends in business demands for good locations. Time will tell.